Groove

Groove

A Phenomenology of Rhythmic Nuance

Tiger C. Roholt

B L O O M S B U R Y
NEW YORK • LONDON • NEW DELHI • SYDNEY

Bloomsbury Academic
An imprint of Bloomsbury Publishing Inc

1385 Broadway   50 Bedford Square
New York   London
NY 10018   WC1B 3DP
USA   UK

www.bloomsbury.com

Bloomsbury is a registered trade mark of Bloomsbury Publishing Plc

First published 2014

Library of Congress Cataloging-in-Publication Data
Roholt, Tiger C.
Groove : a phenomenology of rhythmic nuance / Tiger C. Roholt.
pages cm
Summary: "A highly original work in the philosophy of music and sound, offering
an in-depth study of the nature and purpose of rhythm" – Provided by publisher.
Includes bibliographical references and index.
ISBN 978-1-4411-6627-2 (hardback)– ISBN 978-1-4411-0418-2 (paperback) 1.
Musical meter and rhythm. 2. Music–Philosophy and aesthetics. I. Title.
ML3850.R74 2014
781.2ʹ24–dc23
2014014392

ISBN: HB: 978-1-4411-6627-2
PB: 978-1-4411-0418-2
ePDF: 978-1-4411-7077-4
ePub: 978-1-4411-0138-9

Typeset by Fakenham Prepress Solutions, Fakenham, Norfolk NR21 8NN
Printed and bound in the United States of America

for dottie and les

Contents

Acknowledgments

This book is a reconceived and rewritten version of the project that was my Ph.D. dissertation in philosophy at Columbia. I want to begin by expressing my ongoing and sincere gratitude to Lydia Goehr, my dissertation supervisor, whose voice is always in my head as I write—still—pushing me to think more carefully, less narrowly, more deeply. I am also grateful to the other members of my dissertation committee, Taylor Carman and Christopher Peacocke. I owe a special debt to Sean D. Kelly, who was an unusually helpful external reader of my dissertation; our discussions were pivotal to the way in which I have ultimately dealt with groove in this book. Arthur Danto's response to my first essay on groove was crucial to my embarking upon this project to begin with. Thank you to the generous and kind group of students with whom I experienced graduate school—especially Hanne Appelqvist, Michalle Gal, Jonathan Neufeld, Sirine Shebaya, Matthew Slater, and Brian Soucek.

I am indebted to Ted Gracyk for countless gems of advice, as well as very helpful comments on a draft of this manuscript. For thought provoking conversations about art and music, thank you Garry Hagberg, Christopher Bartel, Jerrold Levinson, Philip Alperson, Michael Kelly, David Clowney, Jim Greenberg, Steve McClellan and Margaret Moore. For my productive and inspiring experience as an undergraduate at the University of Minnesota, I owe thanks to Norman Dahl, Marcia Eaton, Keith Gunderson, Michael Root, and Naomi Scheman. I also want to thank my colleagues at Montclair— David Benfield (a true mentor), Roland Garrett, Christopher Herrera, Kirk McDermid, Dorothy Rogers, Mark Clatterbuck, Cynthia Eller, Yasir Ibrahim, Stephen Johnson, Michael Kogan, Lise Vail, Tyson Lewis and Marissa Silverman. I am also grateful to my many students who have matched my enthusiasm for philosophy, with special thanks to James Owen.

At Bloomsbury Academic, I would like to thank David Barker for his enthusiasm for this project and Ally Jane Grossan for her patience and assistance. Chapter 1 draws from my "*Musical* Musical Nuance," *The Journal of Aesthetics and Art Criticism* 68 (2010): 1–10. Chapter 2 draws from my "In Praise of Ambiguity: Musical Subtlety and Merleau-Ponty," *Contemporary Aesthetics* 11 (2013). I want to thank the editors of these journals.

During my years as a musician, many individuals—band mates, music industrians, music journalists, and so on—helped to shape my views on music and its seemingly ineffable aspects. I am grateful to them.

Shira Gal Roholt, my daughter, has taught me the meaning of intrinsic value. My parents allowed me the space to learn about music (even when neighbors were pounding on the ceiling). My father, Les, taught me to play music; my mother, Dottie, made it impossible for me not to think deeply about it. I was lucky to grow up in a household where a magical mix of music was playing: Gene Vincent, early Van Morrison, Sly and the Family Stone, Frank Sinatra, the Del-Vikings, Roberta Flack. I am also very appreciative of the guidance and kindness of Henrietta and Henry Rosenberg and the entire Rosenberg family.

Finally, I owe more than I can express to my life-saving and life-affirming life partner, Jill Rosenberg.

T.C.R.
Montclair
May 2014

Introduction

It's winter. A heavy snow has fallen. The plows have yet to clear the street on which you're driving but the snow has been packed down by the early morning traffic. As you change lanes you slide just a bit, then you feel your tires settle into the grooves made by the tires of other cars. You have some sense of the firmness and path of these grooves—less by actually seeing them, more through your body. You perceive, or grasp, these grooves both in your hands, through the resistance of the steering wheel, and in your body, as you *feel* the car being pulled, pushed, and carried along.

In a musical groove, a musician, dancer, or an engaged listener has a similar feeling of being pulled-into a musical "notch," guided-onto a musical "track," buoyed by a rhythm, being lifted up and carried along. Drummers, other musicians, vocalists as well, go to great lengths not only to accurately perform one rhythmic pattern or another but to perform rhythms in such a way that they acquire various qualities of groove, specific qualities of "pushing," "pulling," "leaning forward," being "laid-back," being "in the pocket," and so on. Musicians achieve this by playing certain notes ever-so-slightly early or ever-so-slightly late (in addition to subtleties of dynamics, timbre, etc.). Loosely speaking, a groove is the *feel* of a rhythm.

Pretheoretical intuitions

There are four pretheoretical intuitions that can be teased out of the common conception of groove, employed by musicians and music enthusiasts—and they are good ones! In order for my account of groove to be acceptable to those who know grooves well, I believe

I must make sense of these intuitions. First, as I have already indicated, grooves have a *feel*; to put this another way, a groove has a conspicuous affective dimension. In fact, most musicians will say that the feel of a groove is its dominant aspect (one way to highlight its dominance is to notice that when a drummer attempts to perform a groove, she determines whether or not she has succeeded by how it feels). The second intuition is that grooves somehow involve the body and its movement. Where there are grooves, you will find musicians, listeners, dancers moving their bodies. The third intuition has to do with what it means to *understand* a groove. To "get" a groove (to understand it) is not to apprehend it intellectually, in terms of a set of propositions or concepts; rather, to understand a groove *just is* to feel it. The fourth intuition combines those above: feeling a groove, and understanding it, does not occur in thought, nor in listening alone, but *through the body*.

Preview

In the following chapters I aim to clarify these intuitions and to argue in favor of them. Although we are many methodological twists and turns away from arriving at an articulation of my final view, here is a preliminary, rough sketch. There are two aspects to groove: (a) the music (whatever it is that musicians do to create a groove, which has primarily to do with timing nuances); and (b) the felt dimension (the feel of a "leaning" groove or one that "pushes," "pulls," and so on). I conceive of my project as an attempt to do justice to both aspects, and to offer a way of understanding the ways in which these aspects are related. Initially, it may seem that the two aspects go together quite straightforwardly; clarifying the first clarifies the second, in the following way. A drummer performs a rhythm with timing nuances; someone who listens to that performance has an experience that includes a certain feeling that is, *in some sense*, caused by what the drummer does. This is not entirely incorrect, but the *relation* is far from simple—this is where nearly everything interesting hides (much rides on what we say about "in some sense"). Notice that the auditory stimulus created by a drummer is not a simple stimulus that everyone hears in the same way (see 2.1). Grasping a groove is not a straightforward, perceptual task. It is quite unlike holding up a lime green sweater, for example, which anyone who is not colorblind easily identifies as lime green. Music enthusiasts and musicians are familiar with a thought-provoking common occurrence: one person hears a groove in a recording where another does not. In fact, this perceptual variability is something of a musician's pet peeve. It is just the kind of perplexity that a philosophical examination is expected to resolve![1]

I will claim that one can perceive the first aspect of groove (the music with nuances) analytically or *engagedly*. To perceive something analytically means, roughly, to scrutinize an element of a perception in a way that results in detaching that element from its context (see 2.3). If the music is approached analytically, then the second aspect of groove, the feel, remains out of reach. Everything turns on specifying what it means to perceive the music in an engaged manner. Clarifying what I mean by perceiving engagedly requires uncovering a cluster of active, perceptual, bodily capacities and skills that are involved in experiencing grooves, the set of which I later call "the facility for groove" (2.7). Making sense of this facility requires a consideration of perceptual indeterminacy, which I offer in Chapter 2, and it also involves a consideration of the role of the body, which I consider in Chapters 3 and 4. To pique your interest in the later chapters, in the next two paragraphs, I'll offer a preview of what I will say about the relationships among: (a) understanding a groove; (b) the feel of a groove; and (c) the role of body movement in both.

I will claim that hearing, grasping, understanding, "getting" a groove requires actual body movement. We grasp a groove through our bodies. We cannot grasp a groove by means of the intellect, by learning certain propositions, principles, or concepts. And we cannot grasp a groove in passive, auditory perception alone, through mere listening. This grasping involves listening (of course) but it also involves a kind of active, practical, non-theoretical knowing. We come to understand grooves *by moving*. Consider this case: if you know how to use a computer keyboard properly, that knowledge is not conceptual, propositional knowledge but a practical knowledge which is activated only in the moving of your fingers. You grasp the location of the keys on a keyboard *through the movement of your fingers*. Similarly, as I have suggested, you grasp particular, wintery road conditions through the movement of your hands on the steering wheel, and frankly, in the seat of your pants. Along these lines, we understand a groove *through our bodily movement*. I said above that feeling a groove *just is* to "get" it. To put this in a slightly different manner, understanding a groove means to *feel* the coherence of its various rhythmic elements.

A bit more about the feel of a groove: I will argue that the nature of this feel is not merely a qualitative property of auditory perception, nor merely a proprioceptive or kinesthetic experiential property. What, then, is the nature of the feel of a groove? I will claim that the feel of a groove is an instance of the affective dimension of what the phenomenologist Maurice Merleau-Ponty calls "motor-intentionality." Phenomenologists use the term "intentional" to mean our *directedness* toward something. In certain body movements, our bodily directedness toward objects can constitute a kind of practical, noncognitive understanding of them. This is what we were considering in the previous paragraph. I have a practical understanding of the shape and flimsiness of this Coke can, for instance, by means of my fingers and thumb. Notice that our motor-intentional understanding of something can be effective or ineffective (it is normative). A faulty understanding may result in my not succeeding in picking up the Coke; the can may slip from my hand, spill. Now, we experience this wrongness and rightness of our bodily understanding as bodily *feelings* of tension, equilibrium, and so on. This, then, is the affective dimension of motor-intentionality, motor-intentional feel. I am going to argue that the embodied understanding of a groove, on the one hand, and the feel that informs this motor-intentional activity, on the other, are two sides of the same coin: to "get" a groove *just is* to comprehend it bodily *and* to feel that comprehension.

When the first aspect of groove (the music) is perceived engagedly, the second aspect of groove (the feel) emerges in experience for free, so to speak. Again, everything turns on correctly explicating what it means to perceive a groove engagedly. To those who possess the facility for the grooves of a given genre, the music-to-feel relationship seems automatic. This is because the facility for groove is hidden, which is one reason the phenomenon of groove can seem so mysterious. Here is a reason to believe that something like a facility for groove exists and is hidden. Consider someone who possesses a facility for (say) hip-hop grooves. What happens when that person encounters a particular country music enthusiast who, let's say, does not grasp hip-hop grooves? For this country music enthusiast, the music-to-feel relationship does not exist for hip-hop; the rhythms and timing nuances simply do not make experiential sense. What can the hip-hop enthusiast say or do to help the country music enthusiast grasp, feel a hip-hop groove? Most music lovers have experienced this sort of demoralizing communicative dead end. Pointing out crucial, nuanced differences in music-theoretic terms is often insufficient (more on this point in Chapters 1 and 2). There is something about the music you love that you simply cannot explain to someone who just doesn't get it. There is some expertise, skill or capacity that the hip-hop enthusiast possesses which this country music enthusiast does not. This facility for groove is hidden in the sense that you don't notice it *until you find yourself in this sort of communication breakdown.* To approach this from the perspective of musical ontology, I argue that grooves are present only schematically and incompletely in recordings and performances—grooves must be *revealed*, then fleshed-out by active, embodied engagement (4.5).

Additional questions such as the following will propel our examination. What is the relationship between a groove and a rhythm? Are grooves ineffable? What does a musician do to generate or contribute to a groove? Can a listener engage with music in a way that makes it *unlikely* that she will experience a groove? Are grooves features of musical works? Are there grooves in classical performances? Are there grooves in classical musical works?

Why write about groove?

Because it is interesting! In addition, a number of answers to this question will emerge throughout the book, but here are three plain answers. First, a groove is an essential feature of music in many genres. In genres such as jazz, hip-hop, pop, and rock, a groove is the glue that holds together a recording or performance, a central element around which musicians coalesce. In order to understand and evaluate such performances and recordings, we must be able to describe and discuss this feature clearly. All too often, discussions of grooves are vague and misleading. Second, relatedly, an effective theory of groove will aid in communication—not only among musicians but between musicians and others, such as critics, music enthusiasts, recording engineers, producers, managers, music attorneys, record label executives, and others. Further, seeking to elucidate groove turns out to bear fruit in clarifying other phenomena as well. Many of the claims I flesh out and support will illuminate not only groove but also aspects of aesthetic experience, the perception of music, as well as other, similar emergent qualitative phenomena in music and art. I will have quite a bit to say about musical nuances in general (aka expressive variations), and will have occasion to consider guitar timbre, emergent qualities of musical intervals, and even certain emergent qualities in visual art. Finally, examining the kind of temporal, embodied knowing that is at the core of groove can't help but be suggestive for elucidating other temporal, embodied activities as diverse as punching a speed bag, running on a treadmill, and having sex.

Method

Throughout the book, I invoke the ideas of philosophers, psychologists, music theorists, musicians, musicologists, and ethnomusicologists in order to explore possible paths of clarifying the relevant phenomena, and to point out where certain paths lead to dead ends, explaining why, and so on. We will have occasion to consider the work of Diana Raffman, Vijay Iyer, Daniel Dennett, Charles Keil, Eric Clarke, Justin London, Theodore Gracyk, Richard Shusterman, Stephen Davies, Roman Ingarden, Pierre Bourdieu, and others. I offer some interpretations and critiques of these thinkers, but only in the service of the main task at hand. I also draw upon an understanding of groove that I worked with as a musician, which was formed and operative prior to beginning my philosophical examination of the subject. I work my way through the various issues without asking the reader to buy-in to one philosophical orientation or another. For example, although I draw upon the ideas of Merleau-Ponty, and although there is a sort of Heideggerian influence in the background, the book unfolds in a way that does not require the reader to be familiar with nor accept the approach of existential phenomenology—that approach only begins to appear within *answers* to problems encountered in Chapters 1 and 2. We get there, but we are drawn there, step-by-step, as we confirm just how useful certain ideas from phenomenology are for making sense of groove. Biographically speaking, I was pulled toward a phenomenological outlook—away from an outlook situated in Anglo-American philosophy of mind—by trying to make sense of groove. Therefore, it seems to me quite natural that attempting to make sense of this sort of phenomenon leads one toward phenomenology. Only a few thinkers, such as the ethnomusicologists Charles Keil and Steven Feld, have written about groove, as well as the musician and theorist Vijay Iyer. No philosophers have written about groove. For reasons that become clear later, I believe that it is not feasible to build upon these works (although I certainly discuss them). Instead, I begin anew, concretely, by considering a real, musical example (in 1.1).

Although he didn't write about music in any systematic way, the work of the French existential phenomenologist Maurice Merleau-Ponty looms large in what follows. Merleau-Ponty's writing is notoriously difficult, so for the reader's benefit, I will occasionally draw directly from the work of authoritative interpreters of Merleau-Ponty, quoting at-length from the writing of philosophers such as Taylor Carman, Hubert Dreyfus, Sean D. Kelly, and so on (in some cases, their work reaches beyond mere interpretation of Merleau-Ponty, and is employed for that purpose). That said, in many places where I believe it will improve clarity, or where I disagree with an interpreter, I will quote Merleau-Ponty's texts themselves.

In the first two chapters, I draw from my essay, "*Musical* Musical Nuance" (which appeared in *The Journal of Aesthetics and Art Criticism* in 2010)[2] and "In Praise of Ambiguity: Merleau-Ponty and Musical Subtlety" (which appeared in *Contemporary Aesthetics* in 2013).[3] My first scuffle with this subject matter constituted my Ph.D. dissertation, at Columbia (2007), which is very different from this book, yet sports a very similar title.[4]

Initial definitions and examples of grooves

Before we turn to our concrete example at the beginning of Chapter 1, please set aside the preview of my positions I have given above, so that we can back up, and begin again, by considering some basic definitions of the word, some observations made by others, and a handful of examples of grooves.

"Groove" often denotes a channel or a rut. *The Oxford English Dictionary* defines groove as, "A channel or hollow, cut by artificial means, in metal, wood, etc.; e.g. the spiral rifling of a gun."[5] In addition, "The spiral cut in a gramophone record (earlier, in a phonograph cylinder) which forms the path for the needle." When applied to actions or life, "groove" was, in the past, often used in a negative sense, akin to "rut." But in modern usage, when we describe a basketball player, a team, a teacher, a writer, a musician, or a couple having sex, as "in a groove," the implication is always positive. The word is often used very generally to refer to music that is played well. In the phrase, "in the groove," or "in a groove," *The Oxford English Dictionary* takes "groove" to mean "a style of playing jazz or similar music, esp. one that is 'swinging' or good; a time when jazz is played well." (The OED treats "groovy" similarly.) More specifically, as we have seen, a groove often refers to the "feel" of a rhythm, where a rhythm is one or another pattern a drummer or other musicians might play. The idea is that in different performances, one rhythm can be made to feel different. This—"feel of a rhythm"—is the dominant meaning of groove in music, and it points in the right direction, even though it is quite vague.

Consider a few examples. Led Zeppelin's drummer, John Bonham, often makes basic rock rhythms feel as though they lean backward (consider "Blackdog").[6] The shuffle rhythm on Tame Impala's "Elephant" leans backward and is quite powerful.[7] Many jazz drummers, such as the Count Basie Band's Sonny Payne, tend to make their swing rhythms lean backward (consider "Fly Me to the Moon").[8] This backward-leaning is accomplished by striking certain notes slightly late. Rockabilly drummers make swing rhythms, and shuffle rhythms, feel as though they push or lean forward (consider Gene Vincent and the Blue Caps, "Race with the Devil").[9] Ringo Starr's shuffle rhythms also tend to lean forward (consider "All My Lovin'").[10] These drummers accomplish this by striking certain notes slightly early. Some hip-hop grooves feel as though they pull so far backward as to feel disjointed, "fucked-up." Consider the groove on P-Diddy's "Bad Boy for Life,"[11] or the astounding groove of Brandy's "What About Us?"[12] Vocalists and other musicians also contribute to or create grooves. For example, vocalists in different styles often sing or rap behind the beat in order to pull against the rhythms of the other musicians, to contribute to a backward-leaning groove. In a 1965, live recording of the afore mentioned "Fly me to the Moon," Frank Sinatra contributes to the Count Basie Band's backward-leaning groove by pulling it even farther backward through the placement of his notes.[13] Another example of this is Gnarls Barkley's "Crazy," in which Cee-Lo Green pulls constantly against the rhythm of the other instruments.[14]

As I have indicated, in addition to the feel of a rhythm, a groove also involves what musicians *do* to generate one or another feel. For one thing, musical grooves involve an element of repetition. The entry on "groove" in *The New Grove Dictionary of Jazz* begins, "In the realm of jazz, a [groove is a] persistently repeated pattern."[15] However, as I have suggested, grooves also involve slight variations within a repetitive rhythm, deviations from the pattern. These slight variations are referred to as timing nuances, expressive variations, microtimings, and so on. These nuances, with emphasis upon their intermingling, are something like what the ethnomusicologist Charles Keil refers to as "participatory discrepancies." Keil writes, "It is the little discrepancies between hands and feet within a jazz drummer's beat, between bass and drums, between rhythm section and soloist, that create the groove and invite us to participate."[16] (The "participatory" aspect of Keil's concept is active and social.) In *Key Terms in Popular Music and Culture*, Richard Middleton sums up these basic meanings of "groove" nicely: "The concept of groove ... marks an understanding of rhythmic patterning that underlies its role in producing the characteristic rhythmic 'feel' of a piece, a feel created by a repeating framework within which variation can then take place."[17] The musician and theorist Vijay Iyer highlights this combination of variation within regularity: "Groove-based musics ... involve minuscule, subtle microtiming deviations from rigid regularity, while maintaining overall pulse isochrony."[18] Now that we have the requisite background information on the table, we can turn to building our foundation through an examination of a concrete example.

1

Musical Nuance

1.1 Two Beatles recording sessions

I want to begin by considering a real example that will help us to explore the relationships between the two aspects of groove mentioned in the introduction: (a) what musicians do to create a groove; and (b) a groove's feel. I want an example that will aid us in appreciating the significance of groove, as well as the practical import of developing a clear understanding of groove—the import not only for musicians and music enthusiasts, but also for producers and others working in the music business.

In 1962, the Beatles signed a recording contract with a small London branch of EMI records, called Parlophone—this was their big break. There is an unresolved mystery centering on the recording sessions devoted to generating their first single release, "Love Me Do." The relevant events begin after their first recording session. Following that session, their new producer and boss at Parlophone, George Martin, decided that their original drummer, Pete Best, who played at the first session, was not good enough to play on Beatle recordings (Martin would go on to produce all but one of their LPs). This gave the three original Beatles—George Harrison, John Lennon, and Paul McCartney—a convenient excuse to jettison a drummer they had been unhappy with anyway. With Best let go, Ringo Starr was asked to join the group. That part of the story is well known; so far, no mystery. Less well known and understood are the events of the next two recording sessions, which, in Ringo's words, left him "devastated."[1]

Few would claim that the Beatles' first single, "Love Me Do," is among the great Beatle songs. The shortcomings of the song make the groove an even more important feature; the recorded versions of the song that feature a stiff, uneven groove sound noticeably worse than the smoother version we are accustomed to. "Love Me Do" is also interesting because within just a few months the song was recorded multiple times by the three, original Beatles with three different drummers. The factual details of the recordings are well documented.[2] Further, "Love Me Do" represents a crucial period in the group's history: these are the first sessions with their record label and producer, and the sessions exemplify a very rocky transition from Pete Best to Ringo Starr.

In the early Beatle sessions, the music was typically recorded altogether; vocals were recorded separately. Prior to the two sessions I want to focus on, the Beatles recorded "Love Me Do" in June of 1962; this is the session that included their original drummer, Pete Best. After Best was let go, the second recording session for "Love Me Do," on September 4, 1962, included Ringo Starr on drums. The third recording—made just seven days later—featured a freelance, "session" musician on drums, Andy White, in place of Ringo. A deeply unhappy Ringo was relegated to swinging a tambourine.

Ringo's recording was originally released as the single (the 45 RPM record), but a short time later (less than a year), the Andy White version replaced it as the single. Importantly, the White version is the one included on the Beatles' first LP, *Please Please Me*; this is the version that is still commonly heard. Ringo's version now appears only on the CD *Past Masters*,[3] which consists of singles, B-sides, and rarities (Ringo's version of "Love Me Do" fits into the latter category). A quick way to identify which version is which is that while White's version includes Ringo playing tambourine, there is no tambourine on Ringo's version.

Here is the question I want to consider. *What is it* about Ringo's version that led George Martin to hire Andy White? Whatever the perceived shortcoming, it ultimately led to preferring White's recording of the song (including only White's version on the LP, and after a short time, replacing Ringo's version with White's as the single release). Clearly, the difference between the tracks was not minor. It was serious enough, in Martin's opinion, that he decided against Ringo's version, even though the mere hiring of White generated real discomfort between Martin and his new group, especially between him and Ringo. A fascinating feature of these events—the mystery deepens—is that when the Beatles themselves tried to explain the events in their several-hours-long documentary, *The Beatles Anthology*,[4] their accounts varied, were inconsistent with one another, and were often inconsistent with the facts. In the interviews, Ringo and George Martin simply get the facts wrong. The Director's Cut of the documentary includes additional comments by Harrison and McCartney, which are not included in the public release. McCartney comes the closest to getting the facts right. Below is a transcript of the relevant comments.

Harrison says, "When it came to record the record, Pete was bumped out and Ringo was is in, so … Ringo, to George Martin, was an unknown quantity. So, I think he [Martin] was playing safe by getting the session drummer [White] to be there, in case Ringo wasn't any good in his eyes." But the facts are that while Ringo was at White's session (Ringo played tambourine), White was not at Ringo's session seven days earlier. Therefore, Martin was not playing it safe, as Harrison suggests. It seems reasonable, instead, that Martin booked White after having a negative appraisal of Ringo's performance. Here are Martin's comments:

> What actually happened was that when Ringo came to the session for the first time, nobody told me that he was coming. I'd already booked Andy White, and I told Brian Epstein [the Beatles' manager] I was going to do this: I said, "I just want the three others, and that's fine."

Ringo turns up expecting to play. And I said, "well, no [unintelligible]; I've been bitten once [referring to Pete Best]; I'm not going to have that. I don't even know who you are. We're going to have Andy White, thank you very much."

Perhaps no one told Martin that Ringo was coming to *White's* session but we know that Ringo recorded a version seven days prior. So, it is not the case that there was only one session scheduled, for which Martin had booked White, and was surprised to see Ringo. Ringo had already recorded a version before White's session. It seems that Martin considered Ringo's version inadequate before the White session even happened, and that appraisal is probably why the White session was scheduled in the first place.

Here is McCartney's account (recall that this is not included in the original release of the documentary; it is included only in the Director's Cut): "But he [Martin] didn't like Ringo. Horror of all horrors, Ringo wasn't very good, on 'time' at that point—actually Ringo is now rock-steady on 'time,' it was always his greatest attribute; that's why we wanted him. But to George, he was not as pin-point as a session guy would be. So Ringo got blown off the first record." This appears to be such a touchy subject in Beatle history that even Paul McCartney seems a bit nervous talking about it. In the video interview, his discomfort in discussing the issue seems to be what leads him to stumble into the odd contradiction—Ringo's timing wasn't very good at that point, however, timing "was always his greatest attribute." Whatever the case may be, we see that McCartney believes that Martin had a negative appraisal of the drumming on Ringo's version of "Love Me Do."

Ringo's recollection involves factual mistakes but also a sense of how dramatic the events were: "Oh, I was devastated. No—I was *devastated*. I came down ready to roll—[imitating Martin] 'we've got Andy White, the professional drummer.' But he's apologized several times since, has 'old George Martin.' But it was … it was devastating.

And then, we did that, which Andy plays on, and then we did the album, which I play on. You know, so Andy wasn't doing anything *so great*. He wasn't doing anything so great I couldn't copy him ..." Notice that Ringo is incorrect: his version does not appear on the LP (it never did). And he misremembers the order of sessions, believing that White's version was recorded first. Martin adds, "Oh, Ringo, to this day, bears those scars. He says, you know, 'you didn't let me play, did you?'"

Although McCartney gets the historical facts right, I believe he is mistaken to think that the salient difference between the performances of the two drummers has to do merely with steadiness, precision of timing.[5] I will work up to arguing that the principal difference between the two recordings is a difference in groove. Even though Ringo's version is a bit unsteady, the important difference is that he was attempting, and playing, one groove, while White opted for another, smoother groove. (Oddly, the groove Ringo plays is extremely counter to his style.) My point will be that a better understanding of grooves, which includes an effective way to communicate about them, would have enabled the Beatles and their producer to avoid the entire "Love Me Do" debacle. I will work up to explaining just what I mean.

What Ringo and White play

Let's begin by focusing on the first aspect of groove: the music, what Ringo and White play. There are many differences that may arise between two drummers' performances. For our purposes, it is safe to set aside a number of differences, such as the tuning or timbre of the drums. Another straightforward reason any two performances may sound different is that each drummer could make different choices about *what* to play. For example, it is common for different drummers to improvise drum flourishes, that is, drum "fills" (back-and-forth "rolls" on tom-toms, cymbal crashes that accent various beats, etc.). In this way, two drummers may play the same rhythmic pattern while "expressing themselves," so to speak, through their fills. We can set this kind of difference aside as well. The difference between Ringo's and White's recordings is not due to such embellishments. Another reason that two drummers' performances may sound different manifests itself within a given rhythmic pattern. It is possible to play more or less the same rhythmic pattern but with minor differences added. For example, one drummer may add a leading note prior to the first beat of each measure, struck just after the final beat of the measure (say), while another drummer may not add this note. We might think of such a difference to be an embellishment of a rhythmic pattern. If the embellishment is minor, the alteration will not be considered sufficient to constitute a different rhythmic pattern. However, the difference between Ringo's and White's performances is not due to this kind of adjustment within the rhythmic pattern. *With only a few, insignificant divergent strokes, Ringo and White play the identical rhythmic pattern, and when they do, their versions still sound different—Why?*

When I say that they are playing the identical rhythmic pattern, I mean that the pattern each drummer plays would be represented nearly identically in standard music notation. The rhythmic pattern of "Love Me Do" is what is known as a swing. (The term "swing" is occasionally used to refer to the groove, in general, which is associated with a swing rhythm in jazz, but here I mean to refer only to the rhythmic pattern. See note 19.) For the time being, our examination can center on the *typical* "ride" element of the swing rhythm, the pattern played on the ride cymbal (see Figure 1.1). The swing is the most common rhythm in jazz, and it is not uncommon in other styles of music. For example, Tennessee Ernie Ford's pop classic, "Sixteen Tons," is a swing.[6] Many rockabilly recordings are swings, such as Gene Vincent's "Race with the Devil." Some pop and hip-hop

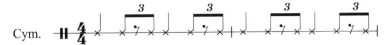

Figure 1.1 The ride element of a swing rhythm. For readers who do not read music and are not familiar with the swing rhythm, you may be able to imagine a swing by calling to mind one of the examples I have mentioned or by imagining a certain series of long ("ba") and short ("bup") notes: ba, bup, ba-ba, bup, ba-ba, bup, ba-ba …

songs are also swings, such as Amy Winehouse's "Back to Black."[7] Ringo and White do not play this pattern on a cymbal or hi-hat, as it is more often played; rather, they distribute the ride pattern between the snare and kick drum. And they do this in the same manner, playing the same notes on the same drums.

Here is a more specific version of the question asked above: *If the part each drummer played is correctly represented by the same notation, how can it be that it sounds different?* The answer lies in the fact that the recordings differ in *timing nuances*: each drummer slightly varies the timing of certain strikes, and these variations are too slight, too fine-grained to be represented in the notation.

Before moving to the next section, I want to drop a methodological marker, so to speak. We have just taken the first step in moving toward what I referred to in the introduction as an analytical approach. We have done this by directing our attention to the music notation. Exactly what I mean by this will not be entirely clear until we progress through more of this chapter. As we turn to the work of Diana Raffman on musical nuance, in the next section, we will plant our feet firmly in the analytical approach. At the end of this chapter, and moving into the next, I will begin to make critical moves against the analytical approach.

1.2 Musical nuances

A musical nuance is typically defined as a note performed slightly raised or lowered in pitch or slightly early or late in time. Timing nuances are just one sort of musical nuance. More commonly discussed are pitch nuances (rather than "musical nuance," music theorists and psychologists seem to prefer the term "expressive variation"). A cellist or vocalist, for example, may perform a raised A-natural, which we perceive to be slightly high, yet not high enough to be perceived as an A-sharp. A drummer or pianist may strike certain eighth notes slightly late, and we may perceive them to be late, yet still perceive them to be eighth notes (as opposed to some other note value). Diana Raffman's account of musical nuance, put forward in her *Language, Music, and Mind*, is the predominant account of musical nuance in analytic philosophy of music.[8] It will pay dividends to consider her view in some detail. Raffman writes primarily about pitch but intends her view to be decisive regarding other nuances as well:[9] "As I noted early on, I conceive the N-pitches [nuance pitches] and N-intervals as just two among a constellation of nuance features, each engendering a similar speechlessness. There is every reason to suppose that musical performances sustain fine details of duration, loudness, speed, articulation, and timbre, among others."[10]

According to Raffman, at the shallowest, preconceptual level of conscious perception, our pitch sensations (as well as sensations of other nuances) are disorganized and chaotic. She has in mind here the earliest or lowest level of conscious perception, at which our perceptions of sounds are not organized in terms of observational concepts, such as *A-sharp* or *eighth note*. Subsequently, our sensations go through an early organizing phase, which Raffman clarifies by drawing upon the work of the psychologists John Anderson, J. J. Bharucha et al., on "schemas." Schemas are mental organizing structures that are formed through repeated exposure to one's culture's music; they are conceived as enduring, long-term representations. Schemas act as grids or templates that sort the incoming pitch sensations into type-identifiable categories. That is to say, schemas transform our initial sensations into pitch-time events. They transform uncategorized nuance pitches into tokens of chromatic pitches, such as C-natural, F-sharp, etc. This is "the shallowest *grammatical* [i.e. structural] level of representation."[11] The pre-schema level is what Raffman calls the "nuance level." Raffman's musical nuances just are those perceptions of pitch (etc.) of which we are conscious but have not yet schematized. Musical nuances are pitches, time-values, and so on, which are perceived at the shallowest level of conscious representation. Pitch nuances slip through the grid, so to speak, of our pitch categories/concepts, just as timing nuances slip through the grid of our time-value categories, *eighth note*, *quarter note*, and so on.[12]

Drawing upon his experience as a musician as well as psychological research on music perception, Vijay Iyer has written in illuminating detail about nuances. Iyer does not engage with Raffman's work but some of his concerns mirror hers. For instance, he too believes that there is a dimension of music perception and cognition that cannot be understood in linguistic, conceptual terms. There are two important ways in which Iyer differs from Raffman. First, he focuses specifically on timing nuances ("microtiming"), rather than pitch. Second, while Raffman focuses almost exclusively upon classical music, Iyer aims to examine the role of nuances in the rhythms and grooves of African and African-American forms of music. We will return to his writing a number of times in what follows. Interesting observations can be found in his dissertation, "Microstructures of Feel, Macrostructures of Sound: Embodied Cognition in West African and African-American Musics,"[13] as well as the article, "Embodied Mind, Situated Cognition, and Expressive Microtiming in African-American Music."[14]

Nonconceptual content

Prior to Raffman's and Iyer's work, philosophers of language and philosophers of mind had been considering the notion that our perceptions are more fine-grained than our concepts. Examinations of these issues can be found in the literature on "nonconceptual content." As the philosopher Christopher Peacocke writes, "Our perceptual experience is always of a more determinate character than our observational concepts which we might use in characterizing it. A normal person does not, and possibly could not, have observational concepts of every possible shade of colour … Even concepts like 'yellow ochre' and 'burnt sienna' will not distinguish every such shade."[15] In addition, consider Michael Tye's comments:

> "Human sensory experience is enormously rich. Take color experience. There is a plenitude of detail here that goes far beyond our concepts. Humans can experience an enormous number of subtly different colors, something on the order of 10 million, according to some estimates. But we have names for only a few of these colors, and we also have no stored representations in memory for most colors either. There simply isn't enough room."[16]

Another important source is the philosopher Gareth Evans.[17] The import of Raffman's book is that she applies such observations to the consideration of music perception.

1.3 Timing nuances

With the general notion of a musical nuance in tow, we can add some clarity to the Beatles example. As I mentioned above, both Ringo and White play a swing rhythm but there are fine-grained differences in what each drummer plays. Ringo's and White's performances involve different timing nuances. Even though we cannot conceptualize the differences (the differences do not show up in music notation), these differences show up in conscious perception (we hear the differences). More than one time-value is correctly represented by a notated eighth note, just as more than one pitch is correctly represented by a notation of A-natural. One performed duration may be a bit shorter than another, while both durations are accurately notated with an eighth note.[18] If my interpretation of the "Love me Do" debacle is correct, the Beatles and their producer were unable to conceptualize and communicate about the differences between the recordings, and this led to at least some of the confusion.

Ringo (uncharacteristically, in fact) tends to play certain notes on "Love Me Do" a bit late, while Andy White tends to play those same notes a bit early. Figure 1.2 shows a more accurate representation of the swing element in these recordings (but still without reference to nuances). We are in 4/4 time; the quarter notes hit on 1, 3, and 4; the first eighth note of the eighth-note pair hits on 2. The eighth note pair is written as a triplet with a rest in the middle. The force of the triplet is to instruct the drummer to divide one quarter note's duration into three parts; in this case, one of the parts is a rest. Both White and Ringo play the same pattern. Neither drummer plays the swing on a cymbal or a hi-hat, as is common in jazz; rather, they divide the swing rhythm between the kick drum and snare drum. The kick always hits on 1 and 3. In some measures, the kick hits just before 3; in other measures, the snare hits just before 3 instead. The particular nuance difference between the two tracks—the one we are concerned with—derives from the placement of the second note in the eighth-note pair, the one just before 3. Ringo tends to strike this note a bit late (so the note is, in effect, moved away from its mate) and White strikes it a bit early. Ringo's manner of playing the rhythm is indicated by arrows in Figure 1.3. Again, the exact placement of these nuanced notes is fine-grained; it is a difference that does not show up in standard notation.

Figure 1.2 The swing aspect of "Love Me Do."

Figure 1.3 Ringo's timing nuances on "Love Me Do," indicated by arrows.

The *musical significance* of the timing nuances in Ringo's and White's performances is that *these variations make the rhythm "feel" different.* In order to characterize differences such as these, a metaphor of *leaning* is often invoked. When Ringo plays the second eighth note late, it makes the rhythm seem to lean backward. When White plays the second eighth note early, it makes the rhythm seem to lean forward. Notice that we have begun to consider the second aspect of groove—the feel.

More examples

It will be helpful to note the relevance of these insights to other examples. Experienced jazz drummers will be very familiar with this manner of manipulating these particular eighth notes in swing rhythms in order to achieve these effects of leaning, pulling, and so on. This is the sort of thing the ethnomusicologist Charles Keil has in mind in the quotation mentioned in the introduction: "It is the little discrepancies between hands and feet within a jazz drummer's beat, between bass and drums, between rhythm section and soloist, that create the groove."[19] Vijay Iyer writes,

> In groove-based contexts, even as the tempo remains constant, fine-scale rhythmic delivery becomes just as important a parameter as, say,

tone, pitch, or loudness. All these musical quantities combine dynamically and holistically to form what some would call a musician's "feel."
Individual players have their own feel, that is, their own ways of
relating to an isochronous pulse.[20]

And further, "An individual musician has a particular range of
preferred ratios and particular ways of manipulating them, which
together form crucial dimensions of that individual's sound, rhythmic
feel, and musical personality."[21]

As previously mentioned, it is not drummers alone who perform
timing variations in order to generate or contribute to grooves.
The nuances different musicians perform interact—sometimes
dovetailing and resonating with one another, other times pulling
or pushing against one another. For example, in rockabilly music,
a bass guitar may play along with a drummer or push her forward
by playing certain notes slightly early. Consider the vocalists of two
examples I mentioned in the introduction. These vocalists sing subtle
variations in timing in order to pull against the rhythms established
by the other musicians; they contribute to or create a backward-
leaning groove. On the recording of "Crazy," Gnarls Barkley's Cee-Lo
Green pulls against the rhythm of the other instruments as he
sings, "I remember when, I remember, I remember when I lost my
mind. There was something so pleasant about that place, even your
emotions have an echo in so much space."[22] Similarly, Frank Sinatra's
timing nuances pull against the rhythm of the Count Basie band on
the 1965 live performance of "Fly Me to the Moon": "Fly me to the
moon; let me, swing among those stars. Let me see what spring is like
on, Jupiter and Mars. In other words, hold my hand. In other words,
baby kiss me."[23]

The nuance level helps us to understand why listeners can be so
enthralled with music that seems very basic from a music-theoretic
perspective, and why musicians invest so much time perfecting
seemingly simple parts. Regarding groove specifically, Vijay Iyer writes,

"music that grooves can sustain interest or attention for long stretches of time to an acculturated listener, even if 'nothing is happening' on the musical surface. A prime example is James Brown's music, which frequently has precious little melodic or harmonic material and is highly repetitive, but would never be described as static."[24]

Is a specification of the nuances a clarification of the groove?

Has our task of making sense of the phenomenon of groove *already* been completed? After all, we have specified, within the general music-theoretic framework, the timing nuances drummers perform in order to create a backward-leaning and forward-leaning swing groove—isn't this an adequate account of at least those grooves? In other words, does this description of the nuances constitute an account of the relevant grooves? Would similar descriptions of the timing nuances of other grooves sufficiently clarify those grooves as well? If so, have we arrived at an account of groove in general? Regarding groove and related phenomena, this seems to be the view of some philosophers, psychologists, music theorists, and musicologists, who apparently believe that by becoming more and more specific about nuances—by measuring nuances with scientific precision—we increasingly clarify the phenomenon. This view is what I am calling the analytical approach.

Consider Vijay Iyer's approach, which provides the kind of speci-ficity one might look for in the attempt to clarify groove. Setting aside his comments about the body (which I will consider in Chapter 3), when he endeavors to elucidate various grooves, he seems to do so by simply specifying timing nuances. For example, in examining a 1952 recording of "But Not for Me," by the pianist Ahmad Jamal, Iyer mentions a quality of relaxation as being in some sense associated with the pianist's microtimings (Iyer does acknowledge that his comments are speculative). Considering a particular four measures, Iyer writes, "In these four measures, the quarter note averages 469 ms (128 beats per minute). The note events in the piano that are displayed as occurring *on* the beat tend to begin actually around 40% of a beat *later* than the drummer's rimshots ... This places him consistently more than a triplet behind the beat."[25]

Does Iyer believe that providing such information clarifies a groove? In places, as above, he does seem to conceive of groove as an objective set of properties in the music, which can be defined functionally. When we provide precise nuance measurements, as Iyer does, have we sufficiently clarified the phenomenon of groove? Clearly, it is possible to measure nuances in the way Iyer highlights. But when we perceive timing nuances in music, they are, after all, perceptions. We must consider our perceptions of nuances, and we must endeavor to clarify *those perceptions*. Raffman understands this; she takes nuances to be perceptual properties. But where does this realization take us? After having just laid our eyes on the clear measurements Iyer highlights, when we now turn our attention to considering *perceptions* of nuances, it is a shock to find Raffman waiting there, so to speak, with her conclusion that musical nuances are *ineffable*. In terms of our methodological trajectory, an even more important reason to explore Raffman's ineffability claim is that these considerations will lead us toward examining the *relationship* between the two aspects of groove, timing nuances and their effects (the feels of grooves), which we have so far glossed over.

1.4 Ineffability: Direct versus indirect description

Raffman argues that musical nuances are ineffable. Ineffability is not a minor theme in her book. She begins her book with quotations from the philosophers Stanley Cavell, Suzanne Langer, and

John Dewey, which she interprets as having to do with art's ineffability. Raffman writes, "Despite considerable differences in ideology, objective, and style, these theorists join in giving voice to one of the most deeply rooted convictions in modern aesthetics: our knowledge of artworks is, in some essential respect, ineffable. In apprehending a work of art, we come to know something we cannot put into words."[26] The main objective of Raffman's book is to "develop a cognitivist explanation of musical ineffability."[27] "To put it simply," she writes, "I want to see how these empirical disciplines [psychology, psycholinguistics, etc.] might explain the apparent fact that conscious musical *experience* gives rise to claims of ineffable knowledge".[28] When all is said and done, Raffman concludes that a central kind of musical ineffability consists of unschematized pitches, time-values, and so on. We can discriminate many more pitches and time-values than we can conceptualize (just as we can see many more shades of light green than we can name and remember). The pitches and time-values that we cannot conceptualize are musical nuances. Thus, Raffman's ineffability claim comes *through* her account of musical nuance: she develops an account of musical nuance, and argues that nuances are ineffable.

To be sure, Raffman's ineffability claim does follow directly from her characterization of nuances: musical nuances are ineffable because nuances are perceived at a level prior to schematization. Our schemas make our perceptual information effable (conceptualizable, categorizable); schemas enable us to remember and re-identify that which they organize. Our limitations regarding categorization are due to limitations in perceptual memory: "we can't name them [nuances] because we can't recognize them, and we can't recognize them because we can't *remember* them."[29] Furthermore, our inability to *report* nuances rests upon this ineffability due to lack of schemas. Raffman succinctly expresses the point in a section heading, "Why We Cannot Report the Nuances: No Verbalization Without Schematization."[30]

For Raffman, achieving the goal of explaining this central kind of musical ineffability rests on accurately describing our perceptual experiences of musical nuances. I want to call into question the adequacy of Raffman's *description* of nuances. In the philosopher W. E. Kennick's 1961 essay, "Art and the Ineffable," he criticizes the ineffability claims of John Dewey, Suzanne Langer, and D. W. Prall (two of the same philosophers Raffman begins by quoting).[31] Kennick draws a distinction between directly and indirectly describing a feeling or quality. Direct description is essentially naming; indirect description involves characterizing the circumstances and context in which a feeling is experienced. (To drop another methodological marker, direct description seems to go hand-in-hand with an analytical approach.) While direct description typically falls short of adequately characterizing subtle feelings, indirect description is more effective. Objecting to Langer's claim that facts about feelings cannot be depicted by language (discursive symbols), Kennick writes,

> Mrs. Langer makes the mistake, often made in such discussions, of supposing that describing a feeling is the same as naming a feeling. This is because she takes as the prototype of all descriptions the sort of "direct" description we frequently give of people and objects, e.g. the sort of description one might find on a "wanted" poster in a post office: "Height, 5′ 11″; weight, 170 lb.; color of hair, dark brown; eyes, blue; complexion, ruddy; small horizontal scar over the right eye." This kind of description can be given of feelings, but usually it is not, either in daily life or in novels. More frequently we employ a sort of "indirect" description which includes a description of the circumstances in which the feeling is felt.[32]

Kennick borrows this distinction between direct and indirect description from the philosopher Ludwig Wittgenstein, who, in *The Brown Book,* considers the feeling/experience of familiarity.[33] Wittgenstein points out that there are different experiences of familiarity. (To anticipate where I am going with this, note the analogy

between different experiences of familiarity and slight timing variations.) Wittgenstein claims that in order to correctly describe a
particular experience of familiarity, we must describe the circumstances or context.

> Different experiences of familiarity: a) Someone enters my room, I
> haven't seen him for a long time, and didn't expect him. I look at him,
> say or feel "Oh, it's you"—Why did I in giving this example say that I
> hadn't seen the man for a long time? Wasn't I setting out to describe
> experiences of familiarity? And whatever the experience was I alluded
> to, couldn't I have had it even if I had seen the man half an hour ago? I
> mean, I gave the circumstances of recognizing the man as a means to
> the end of describing the precise situation of the recognition.[34]

Following this passage, Wittgenstein refers to a direct description of a
table (giving the shape, dimensions, and so forth); he then notes that
an indirect description of the table might be the kind of description
one finds in a novel: "'It was a small rickety table decorated in
Moorish style, the sort that is used for smoker's requisites' … if the
purpose of it is to bring a vivid image of the table before your mind
in a flash, it might serve this purpose incomparably better than a
detailed 'direct' description."[35]

If indirect description can render musical nuances effable, then
perhaps we can reject Raffman's ineffability claim and simply fault her
for failing to consider indirect description. After all, Raffman does
characterize nuances in terms of applying *names* to these perceptual
properties, and as we have seen, she then concludes that limitations
of perceptual memory prevent us from successfully reapplying these
names. Consider this passage:

> Recall the numerical N-pitch names 'A-natural(1),' 'A-natural(12),'
> 'B-flat(17),' and so forth introduced in preceding chapters; these could
> serve perfectly well for enunciating the [representational] content in
> question. … The ineffability of the content of nuance representations
> derives not from the absence of terminology adequate to its verbal

expression, but rather from the psychological impossibility of *applying* such terms "by introspection."[36]

In a review of Raffman's book, Georges Rey expresses a criticism related to the one we have just considered.[37] Rey does not discuss the efficacy of including considerations of context—that is, he does not seem to have indirect description in mind as a solution (he does not invoke Kennick or Wittgenstein)—but he does criticize Raffman for limiting herself to something like direct description. Moreover, he suggests that literary devices such as metaphor could be employed to render nuances effable: "Discussions of 'ineffability' often tend to focus on cases where there aren't single words for the job and neglect the possibility afforded by complex descriptions. Where we lack schemas for nuances, why mightn't we evoke them by exploiting standard compositional resources, including simile, metaphor, and the like?"[38] We will see that such descriptive devices can, indeed, be effectively employed in an indirect description of nuances. My point is that our being unable to employ terms such as "B-sharp(5)" due to limitations of perceptual memory does not necessarily establish the ineffability of musical nuances, because an indirect description may render these seemingly ineffable features effable. Importantly, notice that rendering timing nuances effable, intelligible, does not involve precisely measuring acoustic events; rather, it involves carefully *describing perceptual experiences*. We have some clarity, and we are in the right domain.

1.5 The objectives of nuances

It is crucial to emphasize that a musician performs a nuance for a reason; namely, in order to alter the way the music sounds, to give rise to some quality or element in the music; call this the nuance's *objective*. For example, a singer may sing a certain note slightly high;

we hear the effect of that nuance, a "brightened" harmony (say), rather than hearing the degree to which the note is raised. A jazz, rock, or hip-hop drummer may strike certain notes in each measure slightly late; we hear the effect of these manipulations, a backward-leaning groove, rather than hearing the precise degree to which the notes are late. (Notice that a measurement of timing nuances says nothing about their effects, nor how they are related to their effects.)

An effective indirect description will have to reflect the importance of nuance objectives. Such a description might include: (1) a reference to the nuance's objective; (2) a description of the musical context; and (3) a reference to the nuance itself. Given what I have said so far about Raffman's account, and given Rey's critical comment, you should be surprised to learn that Raffman herself offers a detailed indirect description of a nuance that includes all of the elements I have just mentioned, as well as a thought-provoking use of metaphor:

> Many fine-grained differences in interval width—indeed the most interesting and important ones, for our purposes—are fully intended *expressive* features, as when a flutist ever so slightly raises ("sharpens") an F-sharp sustained over a D-natural across a modulation from b minor to D major. ... The flutist's objective is to widen ("brighten") the major third between D-natural and F-sharp, thereby emphasizing and strengthening the new key of D major.[39]

This is indicative of the depth of Raffman's book; it rewards careful consideration. Unfortunately, in the very next paragraph, before acknowledging and developing the import of this indirect description, Raffman turns back to the task of developing her account of musical nuance in terms of direct description. Why didn't Raffman explore the possibility that indirect descriptions, such as the one she offers above, render nuances effable? What is it about her assumptions or methodology that led her away from believing that nuance objectives and musical context are relevant to rendering nuances effable? I believe an answer can be found by considering the influence upon

Raffman of the account she adopts of nuance objectives; that is, she works with a particular conception of a nuance objective.

In the indirect description above, Raffman explains that the flutist's objective is "to widen ('brighten') the major third between D-natural and F-sharp, thereby emphasizing and strengthening the new key of D major." For Raffman, the important aspect of the objective is the emphasis, the strengthening of the new key. The view of nuance objectives that she adopts—which is the standard view—is that a performer employs a musical nuance in order to lead a listener to hear the musical structure as he, the performer, hears it. Raffman writes, "As I have repeatedly noted, the performer's objective is to mold these fine-grained features in such a way as to communicate his hearing of a work's structure."[40] This is, indeed, the standard view. The psychologist Eric F. Clarke writes, "It is an assumption of most performance research that expression is primarily used to convey musical structure to listeners."[41] (By "expression," Clarke means expressive properties such as nuances, "expressive variations.")

Returning to Raffman, the point I want to emphasize is that she does not take the above nuance objective to be relevant to describing the nuance because she takes the objective to be characterizable in terms of structure. The nuance objective is categorizable, conceptualizable. *She seems to believe that the raised F-sharp itself is the only element relevant to the phenomenon of musical nuance* because it is the only element that is not conceptualizable. Raffman explicitly distinguishes between the structural and the nonstructural features of music; one of the defining characteristics is that structural features are conceptualizable, or, in her terminology, "type-identifiable"—and the nonstructural features are not.[42] Another example of a structural nuance objective is that a nuance might result in our hearing a passage of music in one meter rather than another. According to my interpretation, Raffman sees nothing in the indirect description that can bring us closer to grasping the nuance, nothing that can render it effable, because all of the elements—other than the raised F-sharp itself—are conceptualizable; they can be described in terms of music-theoretic concepts, or terms such as "emphasis," which she also takes to be conceptualizable.

Nonstructural objectives of nuances

Importantly, some nuance objectives are not conceptualizable; they are nonstructural. The existence of nonstructural nuance objectives is, perhaps, especially obvious to those aware of the role of nuances in rock, hip-hop or jazz, because, when it comes to the effects of nuances, musicians in these genres are more concerned with *qualities* than they are with structures.[43] Before turning to the example of groove, notice that Raffman herself mentions a nonstructural nuance objective in the indirect description we have been considering. Recall the latter portion of the indirect description she offers of the raised F-sharp: "The flutist's objective is to widen ('brighten') the major third between D-natural and F-sharp, thereby emphasizing and strengthening the new key of D major." It is thought provoking that the metaphor of brightening is placed in parentheses. The brightening is surely an effect of the nuance, but it is not what Raffman typically refers to as a nuance objective; it is not merely a matter of hearing musical structure in one way or the other, and it is not conceptualizable. It is not what she wants to focus upon. It is crucial for our purposes, though, that one consequence of the raised F-sharp is a brightening of the interval. But what should we say about this category of nuance objective?

Grooves, the brightening in Raffman's example, and other nonstructural objectives of nuances, seem descriptively elusive (they are not as conceptualizable as they may seem at first blush). Have we landed in a *new* ineffability problem? The ineffability I am worried about is not the ineffability of the nuances themselves but of the objectives. Since F-sharps raised to slightly different degrees will make the same segment of the performance sound different: a slightly raised F-sharp in this context may, indeed, emphasize the new key, but an F-sharp(13) and an F-sharp(14) will each emphasize the new key in a qualitatively different way. Music-theoretic concepts are too coarse grained to adequately characterize this difference. One way to characterize the difference in the effect of these slightly raised pitches, which Raffman's indirect description seems to invite, is to say that each differently raised pitch will result in differently brightened major thirds. But it seems that our indirect descriptions, including metaphorical description, will fall short of rendering these qualitative differences effable. In order to accurately characterize the differences in terms of brightness, we will need to invoke descriptive terms that we will not be able to remember and reliably reapply, in Raffman's sense. There will be distinguishable brightenings too subtle to be captured by the metaphors we can reliably remember and apply ("bright," "shimmering," "radiant," for instance). However, next, we will see that these nonstructural nuance objectives do not add to the air of ineffability after all; rather, acknowledging the existence of nonstructural objectives helps us to discover just how indirect description is useful in understanding musical nuance.

The effability of nonstructural objectives

Consider the way in which rock musicians deal with the practical difficulty of communicating about musical nuance.[44] It is not unusual for a serious band of rock musicians to invest a significant amount of time in attempting to communicate about nuances. For rock composers, nuances are of central concern in the creative process. Consider an example in which the nuance objective is nonstructural. It is often the case that a composer envisions not merely a certain rhythm (which is a matter of structure) but a certain groove. She might imagine a rhythm that feels as though it pulls against the guitars to a specific degree. If, upon trying to create this groove with her band, she discovers that the pulling between the drums and guitars cannot be achieved to her satisfaction, the composer may opt for a different rhythm altogether. In such a case, a nonstructural nuance objective matters more than musical structure (a rhythm) for the emerging musical work (for more on this, see 4.5).

Above, regarding brightness, we preliminarily concluded that this nonstructural kind of nuance objective seems to be ineffable in Raffman's sense. But there is a common way that rock musicians move beyond such limitations of indirect description for practical purposes. Rock musicians (and other musicians, of course) share a fine-tuned familiarity with a large number of recordings. By referring to these recordings, they add comparisons to indirect descriptions. They often begin with an indirect description and then, in order to add specificity, refer to an example: "the brightness I have in mind is a brightness just like the one so-and-so achieved on the recording of *that* song." A composer may say to a drummer, about a target groove, "Lean the beat forward—not like the recorded version of the Beatles' 'I Saw Her Standing There' but like the Washington, DC, live performance of the song from 1964." By adding a comparison to indirect description, we have added a degree of specificity to our ability to communicate about nonstructural nuance objectives. In this case, musical nuances are effable enough for the practical purposes of rock musicians, and I suspect, through similar devices, for the practical purposes of musicians in general.[45] After all, musicians do manage to communicate about nuances. Thus, ineffability seems to be relative to the task at hand, and as far as the perceptually rich, practical task of musicians considered above, nuances are effable enough.[46]

The priority of objectives over nuances

A crucial point has come to light: in order to acquire the improved specificity awarded by comparison, rock musicians do not focus on the nuances themselves (the raised or lowered pitches, early or late notes). That is, they do not focus on nuances characterized in terms of scientific measurements, nor in terms of direct description, such as "F-sharp(13)," and often, they do not focus on the structural objectives of nuances. Instead, in many cases, rock musicians are focused on nonstructural nuance *objectives*. This is to emphasize and elaborate what I noted at the beginning of this section: a musician performs a nuance for a reason; namely, in order to alter the way the music sounds, to give rise to some quality or element in the music, the nuance's objective.[47]

In Raffman's indirect description, that which is placed in parentheses (in other words, downplayed) is often the emphasis of the rock musician's practical concern. In the rhythm example, the composer is not focused on exactly how late those eighth notes should be played, and she is not focused on how the listener should hear the structure; rather, she is concerned to convey to her drummer just to what degree the rhythm should feel as though it is leaning backward or pulling. This is a nonstructural objective of a musical nuance. This shift in emphasis is also manifest regarding non-composing rock musicians. All good rock musicians (and those in other genres, obviously) are reflective about the fact that they are able to play notes slightly early, late, raised, lowered, and so on. But their focus, like the focus of composers, is typically on the nonstructural objectives of these minute variations rather than the variations themselves. In fact, in these cases, the aspects of experience that confirm to a musician that she has accomplished what she set out to accomplish in performing a minute variation just are these nonstructural objectives. In other words, the nonstructural objectives—what the variations accomplish in their context—are the perceptual data that guide a musician's performance of nuances, and which confirm to her that she is satisfying her goals—not the perception of the nuances themselves.

For a bit of variety, consider a vocal harmony, timbre example. A backup singer makes numerous slight variations in pitch and timbre. The timbral variations are sometimes controlled by the shape of his lips in pronouncing a word. His ultimate criteria for judging the effectiveness of the variations are not perceptions of just how the lip adjustment affects his, particular timbre, but rather, perceptions of the effect of his variations in context. The relevant effect is often discussed in terms of a metaphor of a *blending* of the voices, which is a nonstructural objective of this variation. Paradigm examples of this kind of timbral adjustment, and the resulting blend, are found in the singing of The Jordanaires, and in Marty Robbins's backup singers, especially the tenor. Listen to Marty Robbins, "El Paso."[48]

Important points have emerged from these considerations. First, the feel of a groove is the nonstructural effect of timing nuances. Second, there is an important sense in which that nonstructural effect is the primary, dominant aspect of the phenomenon of groove. Again, the feel is the dominant aspect of a groove, not the timing nuances perceived analytically (as slightly early or late, or measured scientifically). It is interesting to note that focusing upon nuance *objectives* is not only what musicians actually do, it is also the way out of the ineffability problem! It is important at this juncture to recall the suggestion that offering precise measurements of nuances constitutes a clarification of a groove. Now that we have learned that it is the *effect* of the nuances (the feel) that is the dominant aspect of groove, it would be premature to accept that view. A reader inclined to accept that view will want to carefully examine the *relationship* between the nuances and the feel.

1.6 Wrap-up

In this chapter, we began with a concrete example—the Beatles' "Love Me Do" debacle—which enabled us to lay a plain foundation for examining the phenomenon of groove, while also bringing to light the sorts of practical problems that emerge when grooves remain unintelligible, such as problems of communication among musicians, producers, and so on. There are two aspects to a groove: (a) the music (whatever it is a musician does to create a groove); and (b) the felt dimension (the feel of a "leaning" groove, one that "pushes," "pulls," and so on). A musical nuance is a note performed slightly raised or lowered in pitch or slightly early or late in time (see 1.2). Musicians perform timing nuances in order to generate grooves. For example, in order to make a swing rhythm feel as though it is leaning backward, a drummer or other musician performs certain notes slightly late (see 1.1).

Some psychologists and other theorists seem to believe that clarifying a groove means to specify timing nuances by measuring them with scientific instruments. In 1.3, I point out that when we perceive timing nuances in music, they are, after all, *perceptions*. If we want clarity, we must clarify our *perceptions* of nuances. In this context, Raffman's claim that musical nuances are ineffable comes as an unwelcome surprise. Nuances are minute variations that we hear but which we are simply unable to categorize—we are unable to remember and re-identify them. This is the sense in which she claims that nuances are ineffable. Nuances fall between the cracks, so to speak, of our music-theoretic concepts, such as *eighth note* and *dotted eighth note*. Similarly, one can perceive many more shades of light green than one can remember and re-identify. Thus, this analytical approach to clarifying nuances, the elements of groove, comes with its own ineffability problem.

However, by invoking the distinction between direct and indirect description, we can render nuances effable—that is, by describing nuances indirectly, by describing contexts, invoking figurative language, and so on (see 1.4). It is important that we are obtaining this clarity in the right domain, so to speak. We are not attempting to clarify timing nuances by measuring them but by describing perceptual experiences. This is to begin to leave the analytical approach behind. The topic of indirect description leads us to a consideration of the effects of nuances, nuance objectives. After all, the effects of nuances must be included in an indirect description (1.5). Musicians perform nuances for a reason: namely, to achieve certain effects. In some cases, these effects are structural (to lead a listener to hear the musical structure in one way or another); in other cases, these effects are nonstructural (to bring about a quality such as a harmonic brightening or a rhythmic tension—for example, the feel of a pulling groove). Is there a distinct ineffability problem regarding nonstructural nuance objectives? In addition to the resources of indirect description, musicians manage to communicate about grooves and other nuance objectives by invoking comparisons to recordings and performances. The nonstructural objectives of nuances, such as grooves, are effable enough for practical purposes.

Clearly, timing nuances are not all there is to a groove. Quite the contrary, we have seen that drummers and other musicians perform timing nuances *for a reason*—namely, for the purpose of generating certain *effects*, that is, to give a rhythm a certain feel. In fact, we have seen that the feel is the dominant aspect of groove. In musical practice, the various feels of grooves are the standard topics of discussion and examination, rather than precise specifications of the nuances themselves. This is certainly so regarding listeners and music critics. In addition, it is by focusing upon the feel (rather than the nuances themselves) that musicians determine whether or not they are accomplishing their goals. These effects are not only the objectives of performing nuances in the first place, they ground musicians' evaluations of their own performances. So, what can be said to the person who is inclined to believe that a scientific specification of nuances *just is* a clarification of groove? Once we realize that the dominant aspect of groove is the nuance's effect (the feel), we must examine the *relationship* between nuances and their effects. In advance of that examination, concluding that a specification of nuances *just is* a clarification of groove would be careless.

As we will see in the next chapter, far from being the end of the story, this is just the beginning of what is philosophically interesting about grooves. In the next chapter, we will see that there are different ways of perceiving the relevant aspects of a performance or recording, some more effective than others. Perceiving a groove is an active, rather than a passive, experience. Perceiving a groove requires a kind of ability or *facility* for perceiving grooves. We will see that this facility tends to be hidden. In Chapter 3, I will argue that an important aspect of the facility for groove involves an apprehension of a rhythm *through* the body.

2

Perceiving

2.1 Aesthetic experience is active

Imagine sitting with a friend, exploring her music collection. You notice that one of your favorite recordings is missing from her collection. You tell her that she simply must hear this recording. Suppose that when you play it for her, she is unmoved—what then? Many of us have had experiences in which we discover something striking in a piece of music, only to find that the same music leaves a friend cold. But we don't give up. You can, of course, point out to your friend the features of the recording that you find to be particularly rich: "I love this band's rhythm section." If that doesn't work, you can go further in explaining why: "Listen to the groove," you might say. "I like it because it is so frantic."

If there is still an impasse, in order to get your friend to hear what you hear, you might say something about *the way in which you perceive* the various elements, how they are related to one another in your perceptual experience: "The frantic groove seems to be a collaboration between the bass guitar and drums. Listen to the way the bass guitar keeps racing ahead of the drums." Even after all of this, even though she may really be trying to hear it, she may still be missing it. She might say, "I hear interesting timing nuances coming from some of the *other* instruments but I don't hear what you're talking about." Now you may try to offer suggestions about what *not* to attend to: "It may be that if you focus too much on the keyboard and voices, you fail to hear the frantic quality of the rhythm." Notice that this is not unlike a good critic's attempt to get a listener to hear what she, the critic, hears. As the art critic and theorist Clive Bell remarks about visual art, "A good critic may be able to make me see in a picture that had left me cold things that I had overlooked."[1]

The sound events that constitute music, just as the marks on a painting's canvas, are perceptually ambiguous. Aesthetic experience, in general, is not passive; aesthetic experience is not merely a matter of perceptual reception (as is the perception of the color of a sweater, say). Aesthetic experiences are active at least in the sense that we can, and often must, look and listen to different features of an artwork in our attempts to grasp its various qualities. Perceiving artworks correctly involves perceiving their elements in certain ways rather than others, and this is something we *do*, something we work at. We see, in examples such as this, that aesthetic experience is not a mere sidecar to the phenomenon of art. In a very basic sense, the qualities that constitute many artworks only exist *in experience*. Certainly, this is the case with the dominant aspect of groove, the feel.

Philosophers on active aesthetic experience

It will pay dividends to consider what some philosophers have said about the active nature of aesthetic experience. The phenomenologist Roman Ingarden emphasized the active nature of the aesthetic experience of perceivers as well as artists: "It has to be stressed that it is inappropriate to regard all the experiences and behavior out of which a work of art flows as being active, while regarding those experiences and actions which terminate in aesthetic apprehension or cognition of a work of art as passive and purely receptive."[2] The active nature of aesthetic experience is also emphasized by the British philosopher Robin George Collingwood, who once drew a comparison between listening to a concert and listening to a lecture. He pointed out that understanding a lecture requires more than hearing the noises that come out of a lecturer's mouth; we must actively reconstruct the meanings intended by the speaker.

> Just as what we got out of the lecture is something other than the noises we hear proceeding from the lecturer's mouth, so what we get out of the concert is something other than the noises made by the performers. In each case, what we get out of it is something which we have to reconstruct in our own minds, and by our own efforts; something which remains for ever inaccessible to a person who cannot or will not make the efforts of the right kind, however completely he hears the sounds that fill the room in which he is sitting.[3]

Notice how strange it would seem to record and measure the noises coming out of a lecturer's mouth, and then, by detailing the measurements, to claim to have elucidated the claims and arguments of the lecture. Why expect that measurements of timing nuances elucidate a groove?

Activity is at the very core of John Dewey's account of aesthetic experience. For Dewey, aesthetic experiences are constituted by a kind of give and take, involving a "doing" (an active aspect) and an "undergoing" (a passive aspect). "To steep ourselves in a subject-matter we have first to plunge into it. When we are only passive to a scene, it overwhelms us and, for lack of answering activity, we do not perceive that which bears us down. We must summon energy and pitch it at a responsive key in order to take in."[4] Passively perceiving something is what Dewey calls "bare recognition"; it occurs when, just as a perception is getting started, it is "arrested at the point where it will serve some other purpose." An example of such bare recognition is when I see someone walking down the street whom, after a few seconds, I recognize. My active perceptual exploration of her face ceases once I recognize her. If I were to continue the activity of perceptually exploring her face, this exploration would result in a richer experience of the face's perceptual qualities. For Dewey, this activity is an essential phase in aesthetic experience: "For to perceive, a beholder must create his own experience ... Without an act of re-creation the object is not perceived as a work of art."[5]

The ethnomusicologist Steven Feld emphasizes the active nature of perceiving a groove (as well as its structure of minute variations within a context of regularity). "'Getting into the groove,'" he writes, "describes how a socialized listener anticipates pattern in a style, and feelingfully participates by momentarily tracking and appreciating subtleties *vis-à-vis* overt regularities."[6] The importance of actively attending to, following, a rhythm is at the core of the views of rhythm and meter articulated by psychologists and music theorists who have developed the notion of musical "entrainment." Justin London is a noteworthy example.[7] (I will say more about entrainment in 4.3.)

If aesthetic experience is active, and if a perceiver must engage with a recording in a certain way in order to perceive certain of its qualities, then it will be unsurprising to discover that grooves show up only for listeners who are engaged with the music in certain ways. In what follows, we will consider various ways of perceiving the groove-elements we have highlighted.

2.2 Nuances as objects of attention

It will be useful to begin exploring different ways of perceiving the relevant aspects of a recording by considering what is involved in hearing musical nuances *as nuances*. We will begin by considering comments by the philosopher Daniel Dennett, regarding hearing complex sounds and overtones, and we will consider again the notion of ineffability. Dennett sets out to show that some perceptions which, at first, seem ineffable turn out not to be once they are analyzed effectively. In his essay "Quining Qualia,"[8] he considers the sound of a guitar's low, open E-string, through a three-step thought experiment. He begins by asking us to imagine simply plucking the string.

The sound seems rich, ineffable, and unanalyzable. His method, reasonably enough, is to attempt to break up the sound into parts. Thus, next, we are asked to play the string's harmonic (by placing a finger lightly on the twelfth fret while plucking). Upon hearing this harmonic, "Suddenly a new sound is heard: 'purer' somehow and of course an octave higher."[9] According to Dennett, we have now isolated one of the original sound's seemingly ineffable character-istics, the harmonic overtones. Finally, Dennett believes that when we listen to the open E again, after hearing the harmonic, we will be able to clearly perceive the overtones of the sound, which will render the composite sound that much less ineffable: "On a third open plucking one can hear, with surprising distinctness, the harmonic overtone that was isolated in the second plucking. The homogeneity and ineffability of the first experience is gone, replaced by a duality as 'directly apprehensible' and clearly describable as that of any chord."[10]

I want to suggest that the analysis Dennett leads us through is misleading: rather than simply clarifying the original perception, his instructions lead us to a *different* perception. Dennett himself describes the third perception as being different (in the third perception the overtones are more distinct). He does not seem to realize that in the different steps of his experiment we are listening to the E-string in different ways—and when we do, a change occurs in the structure of the perception.

Figure/ground structure

In order to flesh out this criticism of Dennett, it will be instructive to consider Maurice Merleau-Ponty's discussion of the figure/ground structure of perception. Invoking the early gestalt psychologists, in his *Phenomenology of Perception*, Merleau-Ponty maintains that the figure/ground structure is essential to perception; in order to correctly describe perceptions we must describe them in terms of the figure/ground structure. The figure consists of the area to which one attends; the ground consists of the other portions of the visual field. "A figure against a background is the most basic sensible given we can have … The perceptual 'something' is always in the middle of some other thing."[11]

Merleau-Ponty explores the relationship between perceptual attention and perceptual structure by considering a Necker Cube (Figure 2.1). Regarding the labeled cube, he writes, "When I focus upon the face ABCD of the cube, this does not mean simply that I make it enter into a state of being clearly seen, but also that I make it count as a figure, and as closer to me than the other face; in short, I organize the cube."[12] Focusing upon different parts of the cube changes the structure of the perception. Failing to describe that structure accurately leads to a misdescription of the perception. These structural changes also affect other aspects of a perception: in this case, what we take to be the figure determines whether we see the cube as from below or above. We wouldn't say that these different perceptions of the cube are the same.

Returning to Dennett, he believes that the third perception of the E-string is similar enough to the first perception that the third is simply a clarification the first; this is his mistake. He does not acknowledge that focusing upon different features of the stimulus

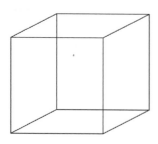
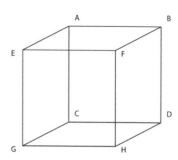

Figure 2.1   Necker Cube.

changes the structure of what we perceive. In the first hearing of the E-string, the overtones were not the focus of attention. However, hot on the heels of the isolated perception of the harmonic (the second hearing), in the third hearing, the overtones *are* the focus, they are the figure. Thus, Dennett's analysis does not clarify the first perception; the analysis results in a different perception; it generates a different perceptual structure in which the overtones become the figure. Merleau-Ponty makes this sort of point in another context: "To pay attention is not merely to further clarify some preexisting givens; rather, it is to realize in them a new articulation by taking them as *figures.*"[13] Dennett does not render the first perception effable. The third perception can be described as clearer than the first but that is not all that distinguishes it from the first. The important point for our purposes is that the perceptions are different, and this difference can be fruitfully characterized in terms of different *ways* of perceiving the E-string sound, a different perceptual structure. As I interpret him, what Dennett takes himself to be doing is clarifying an aspect of the experience (the overtones), which has been there all along. And he assumes that there is no difference between an experience in which the overtones remain unnoticed and the experience in which they are noticed. We will see that when more specifiable *effects* of such subtleties are involved, in actual music, this seemingly minor difference between experiences becomes crucial.

Focus on nuances

Importantly, philosophers, psychologists, and music theorists who examine pitch and timing subtleties tend to do so by characterizing them in the figure role. We can see that this is the case by recalling that focusing upon a pitch or duration variation *places* it in the figure role. It is common in the relevant articles on music perception to find subjects being asked to attend to pitches or durations in order

to report on which variations they are able to detect or to discriminate between. For example, in Eric F. Clarke's "The Perception of
Expressive Timing in Music," he writes, "The experiments reported in
this paper are an attempt to investigate the ability of listeners to detect
small-scale timing changes, similar to those in expressive performance, in various kinds of musical sequence."[14] Raffman adopts this
orientation by engaging with such research:

> In hearing these nuances, we are hearing differences within—that is,
> more fine-grained than—the C-pitch [chromatic pitch] and C-interval
> (chromatic interval) categories. Each C-pitch category subsumes
> many discriminably different pitches, just as each "determinable"
> color category subsumes many different "determinate" shades; there
> are many A-naturals and many B-flats, just as there are many reds and
> many blues. Under laboratory conditions of minimal uncertainty, the
> human ear can discriminate anywhere from 20 to 300 pitches to the
> semitone, depending upon the frequency range and testing procedure
> employed.[15]

Raffman's use of pitch terms with subscripts to denote specific pitches
also indicates that she is characterizing variations as occupying the
figure role: a slightly high F-sharp is an "F-sharp(2)," "F-sharp(4),"
and so on. She claims that such terms accurately characterize
these subtleties; the terms "serve perfectly well for enunciating the
[representational] content in question."[16] In Chapter 1, we saw that
Raffman's construal of nuances in terms of direct description set the
stage for claiming that nuances are ineffable. Here, I am making the
same point but in terms of the figure/ground framework: construing
nuances in the figure role sets the stage for the resulting observation
that nuances are ineffable. Once these subtleties are conceived as in
the figure role, this leads to the observation that our capacities of
discrimination outstrip our capacities of conceptualization. Just as
we can discriminate or detect many more color shades than we can
conceptualize, so too, we can discriminate many more pitches than

we can conceptualize. According to Raffman, fine-grained pitches are ineffable insofar as we cannot conceptualize them.[17]

2.3 Analytical perception and gestalts

The way I have so far described Dennett's and Raffman's analyses is incomplete in an important way. The nuance elements they focus upon are not *merely* taken as the figure; they are also perceived in a particular way, by means of an out-of-the-ordinary attitude (out of the ordinary in the sense of being different from an ordinary perception of music). I want to invoke a distinction Merleau-Ponty draws between analytical (or reflective) perception, on the one hand, and ordinary (or natural) perception, on the other. He occasionally refers to these different kinds of perception in terms of the adopting of different *attitudes*.[18]

To perceive analytically is to take up a detached, third-person, reflective point of view. One adopts this analytical attitude in the attempt to *scrutinize* one element or another of a perception. We adopt the analytical attitude when we "decompose the perception into qualities."[19] Merleau-Ponty maintains that this involves scrutinizing the perception itself rather than the object of perception: "It is the response to a certain question posed by my gaze and the result of a second-order or critical act of vision that attempts to know itself in its particularity; it is the result of an 'attention to the purely visual' that I employ when I am worried about being tricked or when I wish to commence a scientific study of vision."[20] An analytical perception "turns away from the object itself and rather bears upon the object's mode of presentation."[21] We adopt the analytical attitude by focusing our attention on a limited area of the perceptual field. "Now, what does it mean 'to focus'? On the side of the object it means to separate the region focused upon from the rest of the field, to interrupt the total life of the spectacle …"[22] (Notice that this is one way in which perceiving analytically is different from simply perceiving something as the figure; it is natural to perceive something as the figure without separating the figure from its context. For example, when we perceive a certain square in the Necker Cube as the figure, we also perceive it as from above or below; that is, we perceive it as still connected to its context.) This extraction of certain elements of the perception from the whole is what disrupts the perceptual whole. "This attitude makes the spectacle disappear: the colors that I see through the reduction screen, or those that the painter obtains by squinting, are no longer the colors-of-objects—the color *of the walls* or the color *of the paper*—but rather colored areas."[23] The claim that analytical perception disrupts a holistic experience is crucial for our purposes. The "spectacle," the holistic experience, for our purposes, refers to a groove or another nonstructural nuance objective—in Dennett's case, it refers to the initial sound of the E-string.

In ordinary perceptions of music, we do not hear the precise pitches and durations we have considered. Determinate pitches such as "F-sharp(7)," and determinate durations such as "eighth note(-3)," are *made to appear*, as Merleau-Ponty would say,[24] by our analytical focus. We certainly don't hear timing nuances in the way Vijay Iyer specifies them, in terms of milliseconds. Attempting to clarify timing nuances by measuring them in this way is obviously to take an analytical approach to them. Prior to that act of focus, our perception of the pitch or duration (in the normal experience of the harmonic brightening or a groove) does "not admit of [such] a precise classification."[25] Merleau-Ponty makes a similar claim in a consideration of the color of sheets of white paper in various lighting contexts. Under the scrutiny of the analytic attitude …

> the appearance of the sheets changes. It is no longer one of white paper in the shadows; it becomes a gray or bluish substance that is thick and poorly localized. If I again consider the overall spectacle, I notice that

the sheets covered in shadow were not and had never been identical to the illuminated sheets, nor for that matter objectively different from them. The whiteness of the sheets of paper in the shadow does not admit of a precise classification on the scale between black and white. It had no definite quality; I made the quality appear by focusing my eyes upon a portion of the visual field: then, and only then, did I find myself in the presence of a particular *quale* into which my gaze is plunged.[26]

However, the elements revealed in analytic perception are not simply made up in the reflective attitude: "My total perception is not built out of these analytical perceptions, but it can always dissolve into them."[27] This discussion of analytic perception intertwines with Merleau-Ponty's criticism of the notion of sensation, mental representation.[28] Merleau-Ponty includes a quotation from Koffka's *Psychologie* in a note: "Sensations are certainly artificial products, but they are not arbitrary, they are the last partial totalities into which natural structures can be decomposed by the 'analytical attitude.'"[29]

Ordinary, holistic perception, then, is primary and natural; analytical perception, secondary and artificial (but not arbitrary). In his 1945 lecture on film, "The Film and the New Psychology," Merleau-Ponty writes, "[A]nalytical perception, through which we arrive at absolute value of the separate elements, is a belated and rare attitude—that of the scientist who observes or of the philosopher who reflects."[30] And further, "The perception of forms [gestalts], understood very broadly as structure, grouping, or configuration should be considered our spontaneous way of seeing. … Such a perception of the whole is more natural and more primary than the perception of isolated elements."[31] In writing about Merleau-Ponty's view, Lester Embree emphasizes the priority of the ordinary perspective:

In sum, where method is concerned, Merleau-Ponty accepted from Gestalt Psychology that there is one subject matter—"active consciousness" or "perceptual behavior" (a better name could be found, e.g. "living")—approachable both from within and from without in oneself and in others, that in approaching such a matter one may have recourse to an analytic attitude, but that the ordinary perceptual comprehension is prior.[32]

Gestalts

This brings us to the issue of gestalts. We must take the time here to fill out our account in a way that I have previously set aside: nonstructural nuance objectives are gestalts. The most basic definition of a gestalt is that it is "a whole not equal to the sum of its parts."[33] An example of a commonly discussed musical gestalt is a melody. For our purposes, the important sense in which grooves are gestalts is that the *role* or *significance* of the individual elements (the timing nuances, for example) depends upon their role in the whole. "The form [gestalt]," according to Merleau-Ponty, "is a visible or sonorous configuration (or even a configuration which is prior to the distinction of the senses) in which the sensory value of each element is determined by its function in the 'whole and varies with it.'"[34] According to Embree, "Each moment is what it is only in relation to the others within the whole."[35] Thus, attempting to elucidate the *musical significance* of nuances—which is manifest only in holistic experiences—by scrutinizing them, by focusing upon them (as those I have been criticizing are wont to do) is simply a methodological misstep. This misstep is just to adopt an "analytical attitude."[36]

One reason it is important to distinguish between perceiving some element of the music as the figure and perceiving an element of the music analytically, is that we must be able to make sense of the fact that we are able to attend to different aspects of a recording or performance non-analytically without letting drop various gestalts. Surely we do this; for example, we are able to make a voice the figure, or the guitar, without thereby disrupting the perception of the groove.

What I am claiming we cannot do, without disrupting the emergence of a groove (without the groove failing to emerge in experience), is to focus *analytically* upon (say) the degree to which certain sung notes are late. We cannot hear certain notes as "eighth note(-4)" and "eighth note(-2)" (say) while also hearing the groove. We can perceive something as the figure, such as a ride cymbal pattern, without dissolving the context of perception, without detaching it from its background; whereas, analytically focusing upon timing variations (etc.) does just that.

2.4 Describing the background

We can now return to our consideration of Daniel Dennett and Diana Raffman. We have seen that Dennett believes our subtle perceptions can be clarified conceptually, so they are perfectly effable; we've considered the mistakes in his approach.[37] Raffman believes that discrimination outstrips conceptualization, and this leads to ineffability. As I have indicated, like Dennett, Raffman does not take the import of the figure/ground structure into consideration, nor does she consider the distinction between analytic and ordinary perception, and its relevance to perceiving musical nuances and their objectives. When we do take these distinctions into consideration, we see that Dennett, Raffman, and others typically construe nuances not merely in the figure role but also analytically. The distinctions between figure/ground and analytic/ordinary perception are useful because they enable us to further clarify the perceptual structures conducive, and not conducive, to perceiving grooves and other nonstructural nuance objectives. As a side benefit, we take a further step in avoiding Raffman's ineffability conclusion regarding nuances in general.

Let's reconsider Dennett's three-step analysis of the E-string in light of the distinction between ordinary and analytic perception.

Recall that Dennett believes that the third perception of the E-string is similar enough to the first perception that the third is simply a clarification of the first. He does not acknowledge that focusing upon different features of the stimulus changes the structure of what we perceive. In the first hearing of the E-string, the overtones were not the focus of attention. This is an ordinary, gestalt perception of the E-string. The harmonic overtones have a role in this gestalt but they are not heard as they are when they are perceived analytically, which is how they are perceived when isolated, as he plucks the E-string's harmonic. Upon plucking the harmonic, Dennett focuses upon it analytically. In the third hearing, the overtones are the figure and they are perceived analytically as well. Again, Dennett's analysis does not merely clarify the first perception; rather, the analysis results in a different perception.

It will be instructive to consider Raffman's inadvertent example of a nonstructural nuance objective, which we considered in the previous chapter, in terms of the distinctions we have since placed on the table. Recall the pivotal passage:

> Many fine-grained differences in interval width—indeed the most interesting and important ones, for our purposes—are fully intended expressive features, as when a flutist ever so slightly raises ("sharpens") an F-sharp sustained over a D-natural across a modulation from b minor to D major. ... The flutist's objective is to widen ("brighten") the major third between D-natural and F- sharp, thereby emphasizing and strengthening the new key of D major.[38]

Consider this example in terms of Dennett's three-step analysis. In an initial, ordinary perception, we experience the gestalt of a "brightening" (analogous to Dennett's initial, vague E-string sound); the slightly high pitch is in the background (analogous to Dennett's E-string's overtones). In the second perception, we need a way to imagine focusing our attention toward the slightly high pitch (recall that Dennett accomplished this by plucking the harmonic). Imagine that we are at a rehearsal, and could isolate the flute by simply walking toward the flutist. It is possible to hear the flute as the figure but not analytically, to hear it as still connected to the perceptual context— the "brightening" gestalt is still experienced. The next step is to imagine scrutinizing the flute's F-sharp, focusing analytically on the degree to which that F-sharp is higher than an ordinary F-sharp. We are now hearing the pitch as slightly high, so let's follow Raffman and name it, call it an "F-sharp(3)." The gestalt disappears. Next, in the third perception, we return to our original position in space, and hear the music altogether. However, having been scrutinized, the F-sharp is still heard analytically. Of course, this is a different perception from the first perception; it sounds different. The particular F-sharp has been extracted from its context, and the gestalt of brightening has been dissolved.

Now that we have a clear grasp of what it means to hear a musical element analytically, we can see how counter-intuitive it is to suppose that we ordinarily, initially hear timing or pitch variations analytically. When I hear timing variations analytically, I hear them simply as slightly early or late, as off-time. But clearly, they are performed early or late—not to be heard as such—but to be heard in the context of the effects they have, both in generating a groove, and for contributing to tensions and buoyancies that involve various instruments and voices.

Here is the question I have been working up to: how should the initial, ordinary (as opposed to analytical) perceptions of nuances be described? Is there a way to describe the slightly raised F-sharp while it is in the background, in the first, ordinary hearing? Analogously, is there a way to describe the slightly late eighth note while it is in the background, while the groove's feel is the figure? I have suggested that the dominant aspect of groove is the feel; this means that the primary perceptual structure is one in which the feel is the figure. The typical kind of musical perception will be structured so as to hear the "brightening" or the leaning groove as the figure. If the late eighth notes are in the background in that sort of perception, then in order to get clearer about such musical subtleties, we had better find a way of describing those background-perceived timing variations.

2.5 Merleau-Ponty on perceptual indeterminacy

I want to work up to offering a characterization of the background features as perceptually indeterminate, in Merleau-Ponty's sense. I will claim that when we perceive the backward-leaning feel of a swing groove, the late eighth notes are perceived as indeterminate. We can begin to understand this notion by considering very ordinary perceptions. Consider the everyday example of perceiving a house. Along with Edmund Husserl, Merleau-Ponty maintains that when I see a house I see it as a three-dimensional object, even though my perception is perspectival. However, whereas Husserl holds that I *hypothesize* the parts of the house that I do not see, such as the back of the house, Merleau-Ponty maintains that I actually experience the sides of the house that are not determinately presented to me in perception. Here, I am following Sean D. Kelly's account of the distinction between the views of these philosophers on this notion of "object transcendence."[39] Referring to the perception of the backside of a house, Kelly writes, "Merleau-Ponty ... thinks that my current visual experience contains something that is itself an indeterminate presentation of the back[-side of the house]."[40] In Merleau-Ponty's words, "The region surrounding the visual field is not easy to describe, but what is certain is that it is neither black nor grey. There occurs here an indeterminate vision, a vision of I do not know what, and, to take the extreme case, what is behind my back is not without some element of visual presence."[41] Merleau-Ponty also comments on this phenomenon in

"The Film and the New Psychology." After discussing the perception of perspective, he writes, "The objects behind my back are likewise not represented to me by some operation of memory or judgment; they are present, they *count* for me, just as the ground which I do not see continues nonetheless to be present beneath the figure which partially hides it."[42]

Merleau-Ponty's notion of indeterminacy does not have to do only with that which is hidden. In fact, as Kelly writes, "The canonical kind of indeterminate visual presence, for Merleau-Ponty, is the visual presence of the background against which a figure appears. The background, insofar as it is experienced as a background, is visually present to a subject even though it makes no determinate contribution to his experience."[43] Kelly argues that the indeterminacy of a background feature (say, the relative brightness of a light) consists in its *normative* effect: "the experience of the lighting context is essentially normative; I see how the lighting should change in order for me to see the color better."[44] Although I will return to this notion of normativity in Chapter 3, here, I want to emphasize the positive effects of indeterminate features vis-à-vis related, emergent perceptual qualities. I will draw support directly from Merleau-Ponty's texts, beginning with this important statement: "We must recognize the indeterminate as a positive phenomenon."[45] It is interesting to note this contrast: while Dennett does not acknowledge the difference between the way in which features show up in the background versus how they show up as objects of attention, Merleau-Ponty is focused on just this distinction.

Consider what Merleau-Ponty says about the Müller-Lyer lines (Figure 2.2). The horizontal lines are, of course, the same length, but they appear to be different lengths in the Müller-Lyer context. Merleau-Ponty claims that the horizontal lines are indeterminate in a normal perception of the illusion. Now, if we focus on each of the horizontal lines *analytically*, so as to extract them from their

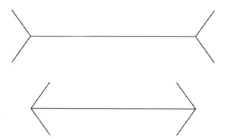

Figure 2.2 Müller-Lyer lines.

context, then we can see that the two lines are actually equal in length; Merleau-Ponty takes this to be an unnatural way to view the illusion.[46] (See 2.3 on analytical perception.) If we perceive the illusion in an ordinary fashion, by not scrutinizing the horizontal lines, the horizontal lines do not look equal. Interestingly, Merleau-Ponty says that they also do not look unequal. In addition to the straightforward distinction between looking equal and unequal, he is suggesting a third option. He says the lines look *different*. This third option will turn out to be perceptual indeterminacy.

Describing the way these horizontal lines look in a normal perception of the illusion is to describe them neither as equal nor as unequal. Perceiving one of the horizontal lines analytically isolates the line; such an isolated line possesses characteristics that an ordinarily perceived line in this context does not. Therefore, in describing such an indeterminate perceptual feature, we will be mistaken if we characterize it as having the kind of determinate specificity that can ground qualities such as sameness or difference in length. If we take determinate length to be a characteristic of these lines in this context (even determinate unequal length), we mischaracterize them. This is what Merleau-Ponty is getting at when he writes, "The lines in Müller-Lyer's illusion cease to be equal without thereby becoming 'unequal'—they become 'different.' That is, an isolated objective line and the same line considered in a figure cease to be, for perception, 'the same.' The line is only identifiable in these two functions by an *analytical* perception that is not natural."[47]

With regard to length, then, the Müller-Lyer lines are perceived as ambiguous. What I want to emphasize is that this perceptual ambiguity is a perceptual-interpretive resting place; the ambiguity is preserved. By allowing the lines to remain ambiguous in perception, the illusion is generated. This contributing to, this fostering of, the illusion is the positive influence of indeterminate features to which Merleau-Ponty refers. We ought to allow such indeterminate features to have this positive influence without seeking to render them determinate. Such indeterminate features are not ambiguities to be clarified; indeed, if our goal is to correctly describe such an experience, we must not give a description of these features as clarified. We must not clarify indeterminate features because this would mischaracterize their role in the experience.

Here is what I have been driving at: the examples of musical subtleties I have mentioned are analogous to the Müller-Lyer lines: the overtones in Dennett's first perception of the E-string, for instance, are fruitfully described as indeterminate in Merleau-Ponty's sense. They made a positive contribution to the E-string sound, and they made this contribution as ambiguous. In a normal perception of the E-string, their ambiguity is preserved. Dennett sought to clarify the overtones by scrutinizing them, adopting an analytical attitude, and so the overtones became determinate in subsequent perceptions.

There is an ancient and venerable tradition in philosophy of seeking clarity. Of course, I am not taking issue with that general tendency. I am, however, following Merleau-Ponty in arguing that, in relation to certain perceptual qualities, this seemingly innocuous methodological tendency can result in misdescription. Here is another way to put this. Dennett treats the ambiguous perceptions at issue as what Plato refers to as *summoners*. In the *Republic*, Plato says that ambiguous perceptions "summon the understanding to look into them."[48] These are unclear perceptions of what Plato would call sensible particulars, which draw us toward knowledge of the Forms (Plato's ideal items of knowledge). From this perspective, ambiguous perceptual properties are seen negatively, merely as calling out to be clarified. Although Merleau-Ponty doesn't mention Plato in this context, this is the beginning of the tradition that he rejects (regarding perception). This history highlights the meaning of "positive" in the sentence I quoted above: "We must recognize the indeterminate as a positive phenomenon."[49] Indeterminate features of perception do not operate merely negatively, as summoners; rather, they perform a positive function in perceptual experience.

2.6 Music, groove and the indeterminate

Before elaborating upon the analogies between the musical examples and the Muller-Lyer illusion, it is important to note that while listening to music, our perceptual attention is not static; it can move quickly and often. For example, while listening to Lorde's "Royals,"[50] I may first notice the way she pronounces certain words, such as "address," "party," and then notice the sounds of the drums, then the backup voices, and so on. What I want to focus upon here are the moments, brief or enduring, during which grooves (and other nonstructural effects of nuances) actually arise in experience.

Dennett's approach covers over a distinction between perceptions that becomes crucial in aesthetic experience. To see why, consider Raffman's example of the "brightening" that is brought on by the slightly raised F-sharp. I want to suggest that the F-sharp is perceptually indeterminate in an ordinary perception of this subtlety. Mull over this question: when one focuses upon the flute's raised F-sharp (analytically, noting that it is slightly high)—in that precise moment—does the quality of "brightening" emerge in experience? If this example is sufficiently analogous to the Müller-Lyer lines, then the "brightening" will not arise unless the F-sharp is perceived as indeterminate, preserved as ambiguous; one cannot hear the F-sharp as an "F-sharp(5)" (say) and hear the "brightening" at the same exact moment. Eric F. Clarke seems to recognize this general point: "Auditory events, or more specifically musical events, are inherently multi-dimensional, and ... although they may be theoretically, and even empirically, decomposable into unitary components, this may destroy or conceal emergent properties of the whole event."[51] (However, Clarke doesn't take into account the implications of this observation for the main work of his paper on analytical nuance detection.)

My claim does not rely upon an analogy to the Müller-Lyer illusion alone; Merleau-Ponty makes this point more generally: some elements of a perception perform a function as indeterminate background features that they would not perform were they to be perceived analytically, determinately. Consider another example raised by Merleau-Ponty that concerns the perceptual effect of the reflection on human eyes. (Merleau-Ponty is ultimately making a point about perceiving actual human eyes, but he makes the point by referring to techniques of painting.)

> It took centuries of painting before the reflections upon the eye were seen, without which the painting remains lifeless and blind, as in the paintings by primitive peoples. The reflection is not seen for itself, since it was able to go unnoticed for so long, and yet it has its function in perception, since its mere absence is enough to remove the life and the expression from objects and from faces.[52]

The perceptual effect of the reflection on the eye is to give the face life and expression, which is a gestalt. What Merleau-Ponty says next is based upon the idea that there are different ways of perceiving this reflection. "The reflection is only seen out of the corner of the eye. It is not presented as an aim of our perception, it is the auxiliary or the mediator of our perception. It is not itself seen, but makes the rest be seen."[53] The idea is that we can perceive an eye-reflection either as a figure, analytically (an object of attention: "an aim of our perception") or as in the background ("out of the corner of the eye"). The reflection makes an important contribution to our perception of life and expression in a face; namely, it mediates that perception; seeing an eye-reflection *indeterminately* fosters our perception of the life and expression in a face. Importantly, the reflection—as well as other background features such as lighting—would not have the effects they do were they not perceived indeterminately: "Lighting and reflection only play their role if they fade into the background as discreet intermediaries, and if they *direct* our gaze rather than arresting it."[54]

Groove and the indeterminate

When we scrutinize a groove's timing nuances it results in describing them determinately: "eighth note(+3)," "eighth note(-5)," perhaps describing them in terms of milliseconds, and so on. This is a *misdescription* of this first aspect of groove. This is what it means to perceive the nuances analytically. In ordinary groove experiences, timing nuances show up as indeterminate features that perform the positive function of (partially) mediating the emergent quality of a groove, the feel. *When a musician's timing nuances (the first aspect of groove) are perceived engagedly, they contribute to fostering the emergence of the feel in experience (the second aspect of groove).* (In order to arrive at a complete picture of the way in which the feel emerges in experience, we must wait for the discussion of the body in Chapters 3 and 4.) As Merleau-Ponty writes, "We must recognize the indeterminate as a positive phenomenon. Quality appears within this atmosphere. The sense that it contains is an equivocal sense, and more a question of an expressive value than a logical signification."[55] My claim is that the feel of a groove (a nonstructural objective of timing nuances) will not arise in perceptual experience unless the timing variations are perceived indeterminately. Regarding the Beatles example, the claim is that one cannot hear (say) Andy White's forward-leaning groove on "Love Me Do" while focusing analytically upon the early eighth notes, hearing them as (say) "eighth note(+3)," "eighth note(+2)," and so on. In the moment one focuses upon the early eighth notes, when they become the figure and are analytically perceived, in that precise moment the forward-leaning quality drops out of the experience. This claim rests on: (a) my criticism of Dennett's analysis; (b) Merleau-Ponty's claim that background features such as lighting and reflection only mediate gestalts when they remain in the background; and (c) his claims about the Müller-Lyer illusion.

Consequently, I am in disagreement with the dominant view that grooves and other nuances can be elucidated through one manner or another of scientific measurement, determinate description. Such methodologies approach nuances analytically. We have seen a number of examples of this view; consider another. The ethnomusicologist Charles Keil seems, in the end, to be open to an analytical approach. Although his "participatory discrepancies" refer to nuances, with emphasis upon their intermingling, as well as referring to the social, active nature of musical experience, near the end of Keil's "Participatory Discrepancies and the Power of Music," he makes a number of suggestions for future work on groove. For example:

> *What laboratory measurements are possible to further confirm matchups between your perceptions and expert perceptions or to shed light on areas of disagreement?* Can we wire up the contact points on fingers and drumsticks? Can we precisely graph the acoustical phenomena and measure actual discrepancies in time and pitch? Within jazz and polka rhythm sections alone there are thousands of possible experiments that would combine expert perceptions and lab measurements to more exactly specify kinds and degrees of "swing" or "push".[56]

In a section of *Music Grooves* that consists of a discussion between Keil and Steven Feld, Keil seems to maintain that it is possible to demonstrate what a groove's feel is by measuring the timing nuances: "There is a lot to do there to demonstrate what the feel is, what the engendered feeling is. Is it some mystical thing? Yes, but it's also quite precise."[57]

J. A. Prögler takes an analytical view in his research on Keil's work: "Searching for Swing: Participatory Discrepancies in the Jazz Rhythm Section."[58] Prögler writes,

> It is important for us to develop a systematic method, an etic grid, for measuring degrees of synchrony and discrepancy between musicians. ... Briefly, what I found is that participatory discrepancies are observable at the subsyntax level and they can be precisely measured. This allows us to say something concrete about swing or groove as crucial elements of musical style. ... My findings may best be understood in the context of ongoing research into what makes jazz swing.[59]

Prögler's research includes a number of concrete measurements of timing nuances. In fact, Charles Keil, who is a musician as well as an ethnomusicologist, was involved in the study: "Keil rarely placed his bass lines or ridetaps after the beat, and this seems to be a feature of his playing. The common element of all lines in Figure 2.2 is their placement before the beat, mostly in a range of 30 to 70 milliseconds."[60] Importantly, Charles Keil supports an approach such as Prögler's. In his "Theory of Participatory Discrepancies: a Progress Report," Keil writes, "Where does the groove come from? ... I think we have the bare beginnings of a scientific answer to this question—scientific in the sense that we can now say how far off the metronome a 'walking bass line' is. ... and, most important, other scientists can replicate these experiments, expand upon them, and challenge them."[61] Prögler's and Keil's are analytical approaches to groove.

Vijay Iyer takes himself to be arguing against a linguistic approach to understanding groove:

> While quite far-reaching in the case of Western tonal music, linguistics-derived musical grammars do not apply well to the vast majority of other genres of music. This nontranslatability is quite glaring in the cases of African-American forms such as jazz, rumba, funk, and hip-hop. In these cases, certain salient musical features, notably the concept of groove, seem to have no analogue in rational language.[62]

Even though his approach may be non-linguistic, in discussions of various performances of grooves, Iyer invokes *specific* measurements of nuances which are intended to elucidate the groove in question. His approach is analytical. Recall, for example, Iyer's examination of Ahmad Jamal's "But Not for Me," discussed in 1.3. He writes, "In these four measures, the quarter note averages 469 ms (128 beats per minute). The note events in the piano that are displayed as occurring *on* the beat tend to begin actually around 40 percent of a beat *later* than the drummer's rimshots ..."[63] Iyer acknowledges the emerging qualities connected with nuances but he ultimately sets out to elucidate these qualities in terms of focused, analytical perceptions of nuances. That is a mistake. Again, the point is that analytically focusing upon the nuances generates descriptions of the nuances as determinate. This is not the way these elements show up when one experiences a groove's feel, and so not an effective way to elucidate the feel.[64]

It may help to briefly take stock of some of the positive features of my view that we have developed so far. Notice that we are avoiding the claim that grooves are ineffable (which is an unwanted consequence of Raffman's approach). And we are also not describing this musical subtlety in a coarse-grained manner which would lead to failing to capture important differences among perceptions, with the effect of losing the emergent quality or misdescribing the perception altogether (which would be an unwanted result of

Dennett's approach). We can render grooves effable by: (a) describing them via metaphor and comparison; (b) describing the perceptions in terms of the figure/ground structure (where the grooves are gestalts, and the timing variations are a part of the background); and (c) clarifying how the background features show up and function in experience in terms of Merleau-Ponty's understanding of perceptual indeterminacy and their mediating function.

Visual examples: Cézanne

Before moving forward, it is thought provoking to consider a visual analog. In two of Paul Cézanne's portraits of his wife—*Madame Cézanne in a Yellow Chair*[65] and *Madame Cézanne in a Red Dress*[66]— an edge of the room's dado passes behind the chair but is out of kilter; the edge that we see emerging from one side of the chair does not line up with the edge emerging from the other side. Referring to the latter painting, Roger Fry seems to suggest that "this general play of slight variations" (for there are others as well) is responsible for a quality of vitality.[67] These paintings seem to possess a quality of movement, which I believe is especially present in a third painting with a similarly out of kilter baseboard, *Madame Cézanne with Green Hat.*[68] I believe that the out of kilter dadoes and baseboards are analogous to the early or late eighth notes, and the quality of movement or vitality is analogous to a musical groove. That such a visual analogy exists is interesting in itself, and it may provide access to the phenomena we are examining for certain readers who are more visually inclined than musical.

These examples may also enable readers to consider, in terms of vision, the claim about the perceptual limitation I made above. In the precise moments during which one scrutinizes the out of kilter elements analytically, can one perceive the quality of movement or vitality? My claim is that one cannot perceive the movement or vitality at those moments. We only experience these emergent qualities in the moments in which we allow the out of kilter elements to remain in the background as indeterminate, preserving their ambiguity in perception, so that they can function to mediate the emergence of the quality of movement or vitality. Characterizing such elements as indeterminate in Merleau-Ponty's sense is an effective way of describing them while they are in the perceptual background.

At the beginning of this chapter, we considered sitting with a friend, exploring her music collection. The challenge was to help her to hear a groove in a particular song that she was just not hearing. Our conclusion here can serve as a practical suggestion regarding such active aesthetic experiences. One effective way to attempt to perceive emergent qualities such as a groove, a harmonic brightening, or a visual quality of movement, is to abstain from analytically perceiving the elements that bring about the emergent quality; allow these elements to recede into the background. This is what I was hinting at when I said that we might try to offer, to our friend, suggestions about what *not* to attend to.

2.7 The hidden facility for groove

We can make progress toward uncovering an important next step by facing a perplexity that has emerged. Surely, many of those who adopt an analytical approach to examining grooves in their research and writing have direct experience with the grooves they discuss; they have experienced the grooves, including the feel of the grooves. One can detect in the descriptions of Vijay Iyer and Charles Keil, for instance, first-hand knowledge of grooves and their feels. I have no doubt. How is this possible, if I am correct that when one perceives a groove's nuances analytically, determinately, the groove's feel drops out of the experience?

One simple possibility draws upon the fact that perceptual attention, and the *way* we perceive, can change quite rapidly; we are often unaware of these changes. My suggestion is that when these theorists focus analytically upon the nuances, they are not—in those precise moments—experiencing the grooves. When they set about theorizing, they unwittingly adopt a scrutinizing, analytical perspective, which is different from the approach they ordinarily adopt while enjoying grooves and their feels, playing music or in ordinary, engaged listening. If this is right, it is understandable. These thinkers adopt the analytical approach in order to attempt to clarify the phenomenon, in the spirit of science—at least one, principal sort of scientific approach, which involves adopting a third-person perspective, isolating, dissecting, measuring, and so on. It is not uncommon to believe that this is the best way to clarify anything. As we have seen, both Iyer and Keil seem to expect psychological and other scientific experiments to be the arbiters of truth regarding the relevant phenomena. At the very least, they invoke such measurements in their attempts to clarify grooves. Their mistake is in not noticing that this scrutinizing, analytical approach generates perceptions that are different in crucial ways—in this case, misleading perceptions (as we also saw with Dennett's approach). This ultimately results in their inaccurately describing the first aspect of groove (the sounds musicians make to generate grooves). This is one answer to the question about how it is possible that certain theorists who are conversant with grooves describe them analytically in their work.

I want to work up to extending and deepening this answer. We have seen that the *ordinary* perceptual approach taken by a person conversant in a particular genre's grooves is not just any perceptual approach. In this second chapter, we have begun to recognize the variability in what different listeners hear in a given recording; we have also begun to recognize the difficulties in helping another person to hear what you hear. What mistakenly focusing upon the nuances alone leaves out is an elucidation of different ways of listening, the particular ways of listening that are conducive and not conducive to hearing grooves. In light of the import of these ways of listening, we might say that hearing grooves (and other musical gestalts) requires a kind of perceptual skill or facility (a kind of practical know-how, which a Heideggerian might refer to as "familiarity"). This *facility for groove*, let's call it, involves some of the ways of perceiving we have been considering in this chapter, and has much to do with the body, which we will consider in the next.

Importantly, this facility appears to be more or less *hidden*. Notice that if the work we have done in this chapter is correct, we have already established that there are certain ways of perceiving musical qualities that are hidden. For example, earlier in this chapter, I described analytical perception, and I claimed that we cannot perceive the gestalt effects of nuances if we perceive the nuances analytically. I claimed that those who do perceive grooves perceive the timing nuances as indeterminate, in Merleau-Ponty's sense. These precise ways of perceiving are ordinarily hidden to the perceiver. The question I asked above is—why do those who are intimately familiar with grooves, such as Iyer and Keil, approach them analytically in their work? The extended, deeper answer I am suggesting is that those theorists familiar with certain grooves who set out to clarify those grooves with an analytical focus on nuances do so because they are not aware of the particular perceptual structures, the facility, which governs their own ordinary, non-theoretical engagement with grooves.

Although the nature of the facility I have in mind will be clear only through the considerations of the next two chapters, in approximation, I mean the sort of facility for engaging with grooves that is built up over time; one acquires it by being assimilated into a given musical culture. If you grew up around rock grooves, listening to rock records, going to rock shows, you develop a skill, a facility, for hearing the grooves, for grasping them. If you grow up around jazz or hip-hop grooves, similarly, you now simply hear and experience them. The facility for perceiving grooves does not consist of propositional knowledge; it does not consist of a set of propositions that must be learned in order to hear the grooves of a given genre (this is why the analytical approach misses the mark). The facility does not consist of certain facts about grooves, grasped from a music-theoretic standpoint. This has been brought home to me, over the years, by playing music with some very well-educated musicians (some of whom lacked the facility), as well as by giving lectures to, and by having discussions about groove with, musically educated audiences (some of whom also lacked the facility). Ordinary listeners probably do not recall a time when they did not grasp the grooves of their favored genre; this inculcation is probably gradual and uneventful.

In section 1.3, after specifying the timing nuances drummers perform in order to create a backward-leaning and forward-leaning swing groove, I wondered aloud whether we had already sufficiently clarified the phenomenon of groove. The thought was that this specification may have seemed to be an adequate account of at least those grooves. And further, similar descriptions of the timing nuances of other grooves may sufficiently clarify those other grooves as well. If so, hadn't we arrived at an account of groove in general? Recall the precise measurements offered by Iyer and Prögler—don't *those* measurements constitute a clarification of those grooves? A person who possesses the facility for rock grooves—if her facility for grooves is sufficiently hidden from her—may have maintained that our work in explicating grooves was already complete. A person who possesses this facility for groove (but is unaware of possessing it) may take explicating a groove to consist of nothing other than the specification of the relevant timing nuances. The reason is that *what's missing* from that measured clarification of timing nuances (namely, the facility) is, for such a person, already functioning, albeit under the radar. The requisite perceptual orientation is already engaged; this person is already perceiving the timing nuances indeterminately, and so on. Recall I said that once we realized that the feel of a groove is the dominant aspect, we must examine the relationship between the nuances and the feel. Even if such a person acknowledges that there are two aspects to a groove (the timing nuances and the feel), she will probably maintain that there is nothing requiring elucidation between the nuances functioning as the cause, and their effect, the feel. Further, even if she agreed that the feel is the dominant aspect of groove, she may hold that this was useful to bring to light, but on the same grounds as above, she may continue to maintain that there is nothing requiring elucidation between the nuances and these effects. The relation is a plain one.

I am suggesting that if a person thinks that there is nothing to explain about the relationship between nuances and feel, she believes this because the very thing that requires further elucidation is hidden. What is needed to clarify a groove, beyond the measurements, is an account of the embodied perceptual structure, the facility for groove. But notice that my critique cuts deeper: measuring and naming nuances is to approach them analytically, and this is the wrong way to conceive of them: this is not the way the nuances show up in an experience of groove, and approaching them in this way will prevent one both from experiencing and from adequately describing the dominant aspect of groove, the feel. Analytical perception disrupts the effective perceptual structure. A successful account of the phenomenon of groove must elucidate the nature of its distinctive affective dimension (the feel), as well as the relationship between the music (the nuances) and the feel. In this endeavor, the analytical approach is an investigative dead end.

It is a commonplace observation among musicians and music enthusiasts that many people—novices, theorists, and even musicians—who hear given nuances, and understand them as such, fail to hear their effects. This is a real practical perplexity in musical practice, which

I mentioned in the Introduction. This is noticeable, for instance, for rock musicians who have performed some of the same songs for two different audiences on consecutive nights. Such musicians might have experienced certain songs being extremely well-received one night but falling flat the next (I certainly have). In some circumstances, certain aspects of the performance are to blame. But even after tweaking aspects of their performance, variabilities in audience reception occasionally persist. Accepting the view that specifying the nuances sufficiently clarifies groove shoves this kind of perplexity under the carpet, because if the nuances are more or less the same on both nights, there should be no great difference in audience reaction. It is for clarity on such a practical perplexity that musicians may look to a philosophical account of groove to begin with. At least regarding grooves, a thorough accounting of this facility, this perceptual structure, will resolve the mystery. Put simply, the solution is that different audience members perceive music in different ways. Certain ways are better than others. When a performed song works well in a live setting, this is due to things the musicians do *and* things the audience *does* (recall our discussion of active aesthetic experience).

Examples such as the one just considered demonstrate that for individuals who possess the requisite facility, there is still something mysterious about grooves. The general mystery is that the grooves a person within a musical culture clearly perceives may seem lost on those on the outside of that culture. Why are so many people outside of one's musical culture so clueless about the grooves of that culture? Those "in the know" realize that helping outsiders to "get" grooves is not easy; some have tried repeatedly with family members, friends, and so on. It is not a matter of imparting a few facts or principles (as I've said, the requisite facility does not consist of propositional knowledge). Music lovers often talk about this problem of communication, in more general terms, as an inability for someone outside of the musical culture to understand one genre of music or another. Some portion of this difficulty of communication occasionally has to do with groove. Jazz aficionados, for example, often refer to the indeterminacies of swing. (When jazz musicians refer to swing, they often do not mean simply the rhythmic pattern we discussed in Chapter 1, which is specifiable enough, but rather a swing *groove*, which is obviously a central component of jazz.) Legend has it that Louis Armstrong was once asked what jazz is. He replied, "If you got to ask, you ain't never gonna get to know."[69] Many things about jazz can be clearly specified. Groove is among the central components of jazz, and it is not easily specifiable. Therefore, it is reasonable that at least one thing Armstrong had in mind was the swing *groove*. Those who grasp certain grooves can find it very difficult to help those who do not.

We have already been engaged in uncovering and clarifying this mystery—by showing that what might seem obvious to a listener involves hidden ways of perceiving, by explicating various ways of perceiving nuances, by clarifying those effective, hidden ways of perceiving, and so on. In the next chapter, the task will be to say more about this facility for groove; this will lead us to a consideration of the role of the body in perceiving and comprehending grooves.

Phenomenology

Before leaving the body of this chapter, we ought to pause to notice that we could have arrived at this point a bit more quickly, if we had followed the method employed by phenomenologists, who have a particular way of beginning an investigation and of framing their targets of investigation. I did not opt for this approach because I wanted to examine the issues one-by-one, to avoid losing the confidence of readers who do not accept the methodology of phenomenology. I wanted to begin concretely with an example, work through more plain approaches, and uncover their shortcomings straightforwardly. The methodological starting point of phenomenology attempts to capture the way things show up in ordinary, engaged experience, as opposed to how things appear when scrutinized. This method often leads to an examination of different ways of perceiving, as we have seen in Merleau-Ponty. This methodology would have also led us, for instance, to the conclusion that the dominant aspect of groove (the feel) should be the target of investigation rather than the nuances, because this is the way in which grooves show up in ordinary, musical experiences. According to phenomenologists, the alternative to their method of examining things as they show up in ordinary experience is to allow one method of investigation or another to illegitimately put its imprint upon the subject matter in the early stages of an investigation. If I am right, we have seen that the scrutinizing, analytical tendencies of certain sciences have, indeed, found their way into what were ostensibly very simple observations of nuances, by Raffman, Dennett, Iyer, Keil, and others.

As we have seen, in ordinary experiences of musical subtleties we hear the effects, the objectives of musicians' nuances of pitch and timing, rather than the nuances themselves. (Of course, with practice, one can hear, detect, these slight variations themselves, but this is not the ordinary way to listen, nor the way to elucidate ordinary ways of listening.) These objectives are what we must set out to clarify. Aiming for a reductive account of the feel at the outset—that is, assuming that one should aim to elucidate the feel by specifying the nuances—is to begin one's investigation *already*, as we have seen, lodged in the analytical approach.

2.8 Wrap-up

A musical recording or performance is not a simple stimulus that every listener perceives and experiences as possessing the same qualities. Different people often hear different qualities in the same music. Musical recordings and performances are perceptually ambiguous. In 2.1, I emphasized that perceiving music is not a passive act; musical experience is active. There are different ways of engaging with music, some more effective than others. Our goal in this chapter has been to begin to identify ways of perceiving that are conducive to experiencing grooves, as well as beginning to identify some ways of perceiving that are not.

We saw in 2.2 that Daniel Dennett's listening experiment did not, as intended, merely clarify the perception of an E-string; rather, it led to a different perception. Dennett's suggested isolating of a particular aspect of the sound (the overtones) resulted in focusing upon them, which led to a differently structured perception (different from the ordinary, original perception); namely, a perception in which the overtones became the figure. Formulating this criticism of Dennett's claims involved considering the figure/ground structure, and the sense in which focusing upon an element of a stimulus ushers that element into the figure role, a structural difference from a perception in which that element resides in the background. Failing to accurately describe this figure/ground structure of a perception results in a misdescription of the perception.

How is the criticism of Dennett relevant to our larger project? Some music theorists and psychologists characterize musical nuances as occupying the figure role. Psychologists, such as Eric Clarke, have examined nuances by studying listeners' abilities to detect nuances. Diana Raffman and Vijay Iyer also characterize nuances as occupying the figure role. This approach not only mischaracterizes our musical experience of nuances, it leads us to an unwelcome conclusion, insofar as our abilities of perceptual discrimination outstrip our conceptual abilities, as Raffman demonstrates. We are led to the conclusion that nuances are ineffable. But it is not merely that these thinkers characterize nuances as occupying the figure role; as we saw in 2.3 and 2.4, Raffman, Dennett, and certain others work with an *analytical* perceptual approach. They cultivate a detached attitude insofar as they scrutinize a particular element of a perception. This way of perceiving separates the element that is under scrutiny from other aspects of the perception. It can be contrasted with perceiving in an ordinary, engaged manner. Grooves are gestalts that depend upon perceiving the timing nuances within their contexts. The holistic perception of a groove is disrupted by perceiving its nuances analytically. The analytical way of hearing amounts to hearing the timing variations *as nuances*. In other words, scrutinizing timing nuances results in hearing them *as* off-time, *as* slightly early or late. This is not the way musicians typically engage with nuances in their manipulation of them nor the way they intend them to be heard. Hearing the nuances as within their contexts is the primary, dominant way of listening.

As a way of attempting to understand just how nuances are intended to be heard, we considered nuance objectives (the effects of nuances). Some nuance objectives are structural, others nonstructural. Nonstructural nuance objectives are gestalts. In a gestalt, the role or significance of the individual elements depends upon the whole. The role or significance of the individual elements of a groove (the timing nuances) depends upon their role in the whole (the groove). Thus, attempting to elucidate the *musical significance* of nuances—which is manifest only in context-rich experiences—by *focusing* upon them, as those I have been criticizing are wont to do, is simply a methodological misstep. This misstep is just to adopt an analytical attitude. This is to perceptually extract nuances from the gestalt. Although he is making a slightly different point, I am reminded of a passage in section 373 in Friedrich Nietzsche's *The Gay Science*. Section 373 begins—"*'science' as prejudice.*" The section ends with this flourish on music: "Suppose one judged the *value* of a piece of music according to how much of it could be counted, calculated, and expressed in formulas—how absurd such a 'scientific' evaluation of music would be! What would one have comprehended, understood, recognized? Nothing, really nothing of what is 'music' in it!"[70] The last sentence is the pertinent bit.

We must admit, however, that we often do listen to one element or another of a song (while not losing the groove in experience). Is that not analytical perception? I suggest that one can perceive (say) a kick drum as the figure without perceiving it analytically. When we perceive the kick as the figure, we highlight it but do not break it off in perception from its context; we do not scrutinize it. Alternatively, when we focus on, for example, the *degree* to which the kick is struck early, that is to perceive those kick drum sounds analytically, and in those cases we do not perceive the groove to which they ordinarily contribute.

In 2.4, by considering again an example raised by Raffman, I put forward a crucial question, which I will frame here in terms of groove: when we ordinarily experience a groove, we do not hear the timing nuances analytically, and we often do not hear the timing nuances as the figure. How do these timing nuances show up in an experience of a groove when they remain in the background? The key to addressing this question, which I discuss in 2.5, is Merleau-Ponty's notion of perceptual indeterminacy. Certain aspects of a perception are not perceived analytically, and they do not occupy the figure role in a perception; they lie in the background. Such background features, while not perceived with specificity, still have an influence on what we perceive. For example, when we are gripped by the illusion of the Müller-Lyer lines, the horizontal lines are not perceived with specificity; the horizontal lines show up in this perception as ambiguous with respect to length. Another example is the overtones in an ordinary perception of an E-string. Overtones are not perceived with specificity in such a perception but they certainly have an effect upon the perceived sound of the string. They are ambiguously present in the perception; they are indeterminate.

In 2.6, I argue for the importance of the effects of indeterminate features in perception. Certain elements of certain perceptions perform a function as indeterminate that they would not perform were they to be perceived determinately. Merleau-Ponty's discussion of the reflections in eyes bears this out. Over time, painters discovered that adding reflections to eyes enlivens a face. If we scrutinize these reflections in eyes, perceive them analytically, render them determinate, this quality disappears in that moment. In order to foster the gestalt of enlivening, the reflections must be perceived indeterminately. The situation is similar regarding groove: describing the timing variations determinately—as, for instance, "eighth note(+3)" or "eighth note(-5)"—results in a misdescription of the experience of a groove. In an ordinary experience of a groove, the timing nuances are perceived as indeterminate and foster the groove's feel. I claim that the timing nuances *must* be perceived in this way in order for the groove's feel to emerge in experience. This claim is supported by criticisms of analytical approaches as well as by Merleau-Ponty's claim that background features such as a lighting context and reflection only mediate gestalts when they remain in the background. This is also explored in 2.6 through a visual example of nuances and indeterminacy drawn from three related paintings by Cézanne.

Note that my view implies that certain scientific examinations of timing nuances miss the mark, where these approaches treat nuances analytically, as determinate. Also notice that my approach does not treat grooves in too coarse-grained of a manner (an approach such as Dennett's would). My approach also avoids a conclusion that grooves are ineffable (an approach such as Raffman's would result in this conclusion). Ineffability can be avoided by describing grooves metaphorically and by invoking comparisons (see 1.5). In this chapter, we saw that further clarity can be won by invoking the figure/ground structure (where the grooves are gestalts, and the timing nuances are a part of the background). Further, the notion of indeterminacy enables us to elucidate how the background features show up and function in these groove experiences. At the end of 2.6,

I parlay my view into a simple, practical suggestion for attempting to listen, musically, to grooves and other nuance-effects: abstain from analytically perceiving the elements that foster the emergent quality in question; allow these elements to remain ambiguous, indeterminate, to recede into the background. This practical suggestion, however, is incomplete until we explore the role of the body in the next chapter.

In 2.7 I point out that it is common to be unaware of the details of the perceptual approach one adopts. We can, perhaps, detect this lack of awareness in the psychologists I have mentioned, who investigate the perception of musical nuances. They do not seem to realize that when they ask subjects to listen in order to detect slight differences in pitch (e.g.), they are leading the subjects to perceive the music analytically (they certainly do not acknowledge that this can lead to the problems I have outlined). Consequently, a person who adopts an analytical view is likely to leave out of her account altogether a consideration of ways of perceiving. We have already stressed the importance of some of these perceptual ways and the effect on how features show up in perception: analytical versus engaged, determinate versus indeterminate, and so on.

Since these ways of perceiving are so central to my account, and since I will go on, in the next chapter, to add to these ways a relevant role of the body in perceiving grooves, I find it helpful to characterize the set of perceptual ways and bodily comportments that are conducive to perceiving grooves as a *facility for groove*. I understand this facility to be a kind of skill or know-how for engaging with grooves. I have argued that, both to those who possess it, and to those who do not, the facility for groove tends to be hidden. This facility is built up over time, through being assimilated into a particular musical culture. It does not consist of a set of facts, propositions, or principles about grooves. Note the implication of this hiddenness: a person who is unaware of possessing the facility may not realize just what work must be done to clarify groove in general (or particular grooves) because her facility for groove, and all this contains, is hidden from her. This hiddenness may result in her understanding the explication of groove to consist of nothing other than the specification of the relevant timing nuances. This is what appears to be the case regarding some thinkers we have considered, who seem preoccupied with measuring nuances.

However, those who possess the facility for groove, but are unaware of it, still acknowledge a certain mystery about grooves. For listeners outside of a given musical culture, it can be difficult to come to grasp the grooves within it. And it can be quite difficult for those inside the culture to help those outside the culture to grasp the grooves (note that if the facility for groove consisted of propositional knowledge, imparting this assistance would be more straightforward). We have already been engaged in uncovering and clarifying this mystery by examining different ways of perceiving nuances, and so on. The elucidation continues in the next chapter with a focus on the role of the body.

3

The Body

3.1 Music and the body

I mentioned at the outset that one common, pretheoretical intuition about grooves is that they somehow involve the body and its movement. Where there are grooves, we find musicians, listeners, and dancers moving their bodies. Another common intuition is that "getting" a groove, understanding it, has something to do with the body. Also, the feel of a groove is thought to be, in some sense, a bodily feel. It is obvious that many of the metaphors that refer to the feels of grooves have to do with the body: leaning, pushing, pulling, being lifted up (buoyancy), and so on. These body-rhythm connections do not come out of nowhere; the connections between music, in general, and the body, are ancient and deep. One way to highlight the ancient relationship between music and the body is by noting the relationship between music and dance. Music and dance were deeply integrated, for instance, in a number of musical styles in ancient Greece. As Thomas Mathiesen writes, "In the dithyramb, partheneion, and hyporcheme, the relationship of dance and music was especially prominent; but the most complete union of music, text, movement, and costume was developed in the drama which formed a centerpiece of the civic and religious festivals of the Greeks."[1] The very medium of dance is, of course, the human body.

Bruce Baugh was one of the first philosophers of art to write seriously about rock music. In 1993, he emphasized the role of the body in relation to rock music in general. In his "Prolegomena to

Any Aesthetics of Rock Music," he argues that rock music requires a different aesthetic theory from the genre typically considered in aesthetics (namely, classical music). Baugh characterized traditional aesthetic theory as emphasizing form over matter, and argued that rock can be neither understood nor evaluated in those terms.[2] Interestingly, Baugh claims that rock music is essentially visceral.[3] Stephen Davies makes a critical point against Baugh that is useful for our purposes. He considers Baugh's essay in his "Rock Versus Classical Music."[4] Davies claims that, in our encounters with music, "visceral responses" are even more prevalent than we realize. This is not merely the case regarding rock or popular music; visceral responses are ubiquitous in encounters with classical music as well. Davies writes, "Music's regularities and its cross-patterns are echoed kinesthetically by both the performer and the listener, who twitch, tap, contract, flex, twist, jerk, tense, sway, and stretch as they react bodily to the music. Music moves us, quite literally, and often we are unaware of the small motions we make in response to it."[5] "All music," Davies writes, "classical as much as other kinds, *produces* a visceral response in those who are familiar with, and who enjoy, its style and idiom."[6]

It is thought provoking that Davies characterizes this visceral dimension as resting on *responses* that music *causes*. I do not doubt that music's *causing* movement is one way in which music relates to the body. But it is important to highlight this view because it is often assumed that this is the only way in which the body and music are related. That is, music's relationship to the body is typically conceived in the terms Davies implies: music is a *cause*; body movement is an *effect*. The cause/effect relationship is often referred to in discussing music and dance: some music makes one want to dance; other music does not. Contrary to this, we will see that this cause/effect relationship is not the interesting or illuminating relationship between music and the body for our purposes.

3.2 Body movement

We need to think more carefully about the relationship between music and body movement. There are plenty of bodily movements in the activities of musicians. Musicians engage in different kinds of movement. Considering their movements will help to draw out the particular kind of movement that is not only relevant to performing but also central to perceiving and understanding grooves. First, there is an obvious, instrumental sense in which musicians move their bodies in order to make music. A guitarist moves his fingers on both hands in order to manipulate the strings. A drummer aims for her kick drum to sound on the first and third beat of each measure, so she maneuvers her leg, ankle, foot, and toes to bring this about. Clearly these movements are not merely caused by the music; these are purposive actions.

A second kind of movement consists of those which, on the surface, seem to be superfluous. Consider the example of a drummer playing eighth notes on hi-hat cymbals. Imagine that she moves her arm in a large motion with every other strike, while she plays the in-between notes with wrist movements alone. This sweeping, quarter-note arm movement might seem unnecessary, since she could simply strike all of the notes via wrist movement alone. An *ineffective* drum teacher, on a principle of the economy of movement, might encourage her students, in such a case, only to move their wrists. But these quarter-note arm movements are actually an effective aspect of a drummer's technique, in that they lead to a smooth accentuation of the quarter notes. Ringo Starr invoked this kind of quarter-note movement in playing shuffle rhythms, and this contributes to the smoothness and forward-leaning quality of his shuffles (the version of "Love Me Do" that we considered is an outlier). It is for this reason that better and more subtle drum teachers will often teach accent patterns by instructing students on how to move their bodies rather than on how hard to hit which drum and when to do so. An example: consider a common, rock snare drum pattern that includes a strike on 2, as well as on the "and" of 2, and on 4. In working on improving my performance of this beat, a drum teacher (Elliot Fine) once instructed me to drop my left elbow on the "and" of 2 in each measure. He was attempting to get me to accent that beat. This movement achieved that objective more smoothly than telling me directly to accent the strike (it didn't disrupt my other movements but merely changed the emphasis by means of a shift in the body). These movements of technique are also, clearly, not caused by the music; they are purposive.

A third kind of musicians' movement often does not involve the limbs that actually create the sound with the instrument. (This kind of movement will serve as a wedge into the kind of movement that relates to perception and understanding grooves, which I ultimately want to focus upon.) Musicians—and listeners, as Davies highlights—move their heads, hips, legs, tap their feet, and so on. A rock guitarist such as The Clash's Joe Strummer slams his heel into the ground in time with the rhythm's pulse. Jazz/pop singers such as Frank Sinatra or Louis Prima often snap their fingers while singing. Ringo Starr famously sways his head from side to side. A drummer may also move her shoulders; a bassist may move his neck forward and backward. This sort of movement is not directly related to making music.

This third category of movement typically involves moving to the music's pulse or tactus. Pulsations are "regularly recurring articulations in the flow of musical time."[7] Nearly all music has a pulse, or tactus. Fred Lerdahl and Ray Jackendoff define "tactus" as "the level of beats that is conducted and with which one most naturally coordinates foot-tapping and dance steps."[8] The pulse is typically sounded, but it can also be present implicitly. A pulse can be constituted by one or more musical elements, as the philosopher of music Lee Brown writes, about jazz, "By some means or other, whether through the efforts of the rhythm section, the pianist's left hand, or some other device, jazz music provides an underlying pulsation."[9] Regarding the cases we are considering, the pulse is specified in the time signature as consisting of four quarter notes per measure.

Are these movements simply *reactions* to the music? This may seem to be what is occurring. This way of understanding such movements would be in line with Davies's comments in 3.1, the idea being that music's relationship to the body is typically conceived in terms of a cause (the music) and effects (movements of the body). We might suppose, that is, that these movements are not made by musicians in order to achieve certain results but are simply movements caused by the music. Contrary to this view, music teachers know that foot-tapping (say) does aid a musician in "keeping time," or in grasping a tune's rhythm. Moving some part of their bodies in order to keep time is something musicians *do*, not something occurring simply because it is done to the musicians by the music. What I want to suggest is that this sort of movement is not merely an aid to playing but a part of the listening process. Such movement helps a musician to hear—or better, to grasp—a rhythm. This is a principal reason it serves as an aid in playing music. If such movement helps a musician to hear or grasp a rhythm, we can expect that some *listeners* will also move in this way, for this same reason. If this is right, then this will be a kind of movement *in listening* that is not a mere effect of the music. This general sort of movement—moving to the music's pulse in order to grasp the rhythm—is what I will begin to explore below.

3.3 Vijay Iyer

We have seen in previous chapters that the musician and theorist Vijay Iyer touches on important issues regarding the phenomenon of groove. It is obvious that he has an informed, first-hand acquaintance with grooves, and he invokes thought-provoking insights from the work of a number of psychologists and music theorists. My primary goals in this section are to use the nudge Iyer's work provides to think even more about the body's relevance to groove, and also to further clarify the differences between our views. As I have argued in previous chapters, one way in which Iyer's view differs from mine is that he is among those who approach timing nuances analytically. That is, while he acknowledges the qualities that emerge from timing nuances, he ultimately sets out to elucidate these qualities in terms of focused, analytical perceptions of nuances, which characterize the nuances as determinate (recall the detailed measurements of timing nuances that he presents). This is not the way these elements show up in ordinary experiences of grooves, so this is not an effective way to elucidate grooves or their feels. In this section, I want to critically examine Iyer's attempt to characterize groove as embodied.

The title of Iyer's principal article is, "Embodied Mind, Situated Cognition, and Expressive Microtiming in African-American Music." In the article, Iyer says that he is considering groove from the perspective of embodied cognition, which "treats cognition as an activity."[10] I want to suggest that he does not offer, nor lay a foundation for, a truly active, embodied account of groove. As he correctly states, "The embodiment hypothesis suggests an alternative basis for cognitive processes. Perception is understood as *perceptually guided action*."[11] Iyer offers some promising thoughts about embodied cognition but I want to suggest that he sets off down the wrong path to effectively follow through on the promise. The research Iyer does apply to groove, while it examines the role in rhythm perception of certain neural systems and psychological processes *involved* in body movement, it does not consider the role of *actual* body movement in rhythm perception and apprehension (I will suggest in subsequent sections that this is essential to explaining groove).[12]

Iyer draws upon the work of psychologists who trace connections between mental representations of rhythm and mental representations of bodily movement. (I suspect that these psychologists are using the term "representation" too loosely; nevertheless, at the very least, they are referring to neural processes typically involved in body movement, not body movement itself.) These psychologists are not discussing actual body movement but something more like imagined movement.[13] For example, Iyer appeals to research by N. P. M. Todd, who writes, "[I]f the spatiotemporal form of certain [sensory] stimuli are matched to the dynamics of the motor system, then they may evoke a motion of an internal representation, or motor image, of the corresponding synergetic elements of the musculoskeletal system, *even if the musculoskeletal system itself does not move*."[14] Drawing upon such research does not enable Iyer to make good on his aspiration to describe truly active, embodied rhythm perception. Iyer concludes, "Hence, the act of listening to rhythmic music involves the same *mental processes* that generate bodily motion."[15] The important point for our purposes is, as Iyer writes, "In the sensorimotor perspective, a perceived rhythm is literally an *imagined* movement."[16] The contrast between Iyer's approach and mine will be stark in the next sections, as I focus on actual body movement. (I will turn to Iyer's claims relating to entrainment in 4.2, once my view is on the table.)

Although we part ways in the above, crucial sense, Iyer's emphasis on the body and its general relevance to groove supports my placing the body at the center of my account. Consequently, to further motivate my approach, in the remainder of this section I will relate a few of Iyer's observations about the connections between groove and the body. One way in which he attempts to emphasize the connection is by suggesting that certain kinds of rhythms resonate with or correlate to bodily activities that are typically considered nonmusical (in doing so, he draws upon the psychological research of Paul Fraisse and N. P. M. Todd).[17] As an example, he suggests, "tactus-heavy urban dance music often makes sonic references to foot-stomping and to sexually suggestive slapping of skin."[18] Iyer also notes possible bodily resonances between certain grooves and certain social behaviors. For example, he suggests, again drawing upon psychological research, that some timing nuances involved in a particular groove (a backbeat) are similar to the stomping and clapping of a particular sort of religious dance. "Though these arguments are quite speculative, it is plausible that there is an important relationship between the backbeat and the body, informed by the African-American cultural model of the ring shout."[19] I don't doubt that there is something to these speculations but what is needed is an account of embodied perception that helps to elucidate the connections, as well as the role of actual body movement in perceiving grooves.

Iyer does consider the role of actual body movement in the case of musicians *playing* grooves. Iyer quotes jazz trumpeter Doc Cheatham: "'[Playing]'s like dancing; it's the movement of the body that inspires you to play. You have to pat your foot; you get a different feeling altogether than when you play not patting your foot.' Here he is speaking not of tapping the rhythm he is playing, but tapping the underlying pulse in contrast to what he is playing."[20] Again, importantly, what Iyer does not consider is the role of movement in perceiving and in coming to understand grooves. As I have mentioned, I will claim that when musicians move, their movement is not merely for the purpose of creating grooves but also for the purpose of perceiving them, grasping them, as a prerequisite for contributing to them or creating them.

What we need is an underlying view of the body's role in perception that helps to elucidate this role of body movement in groove. Below, I will argue that we can discover just how: (a) body movement; (b) a groove's feel; and (c) the understanding of a groove are integrated. We can make sense of this if we conceive of perception as essentially embodied, in a sense that goes beyond considering merely the neural systems and processes associated with bodily movement. We must consider the role of actual body movement in the experience and understanding of grooves, not just the movement of musicians but of listeners as well.

3.4 Motor intentionality: Merleau-Ponty

We are aiming to clarify the role of the body in groove, as well as the nature of the feel of grooves. Merleau-Ponty is the original source for contemporary views of embodied perception. Considering his account of perception in general, including as it does an emphasis on the body's role in perception, will enable us to explicate what is missing in our account of groove. In this section, we will work up to exploring the role of body movement in perception.

The traditional view of perception

Merleau-Ponty is critical of the dominant, representational view of perception. This dominant view is shared by (with variations of course) rationalists such as René Descartes, subsequent contemporary cognitivists, computationalists, as well as empiricists such as John Locke and David Hume. According to this traditional view, when I perceive (say) a chocolate soufflé, I am not directly aware of the soufflé; rather, I am directly aware of an internal representation. Different philosophers conceive of and refer to these inner, mental items in different terms: "ideas," "impressions," "sense-data," and so on).[21]

According to this traditional view, our representations and the objects in our environments are related causally; internal representations are caused by external stimuli. As Lawrence Hass describes Descartes's view, "It is the view that perception is 'built up' out of discrete sensations causally activated from 'outside,' that perception is an internal mental representation or subjective appearance of an external, essentially mechanistic physical reality."[22] When a waiter places a chocolate soufflé on my table, the soufflé causes a representation (I am leaving out the details concerning light and reflectance for simplicity's sake). Seeing the soufflé *just is* to have the representation. Thus, we perceive what is outside of us indirectly, by means of internal representations; perception, on this view, is a mental, inner, subjective phenomenon.

The body, on this traditional view, is simply a cog in this causal process. Most straightforwardly, some parts of my body occupy a causal role as input mechanisms leading to representations, such as rods and cones (of course, Descartes did not have the "rod" and "cone" concepts). As Taylor Carman writes, "For Descartes and the tradition that followed him, the body is just that chunk of the physical world that happens to be causally contiguous with the soul, the last link in a chain of causes and effects that ends with the perceptual experience."[23] Note that even on the traditional view, my body can function as an active instrument of perception, albeit mechanistically. For example, I may get up and walk around the corner in order to see who is speaking in the next room, I may cup my ear with my hand in order to hear better, and so on. Importantly, this role of the body in perception, on the representational view of perception, is explainable in terms of causes and effects.

Now, in this context, from within the tradition that adopts this view of perception, when we ask—why do people move in the presence of music? It is unsurprising that Stephen Davies answers as he does. Since the standard body and perception relations are cause and effect relations, it stands to reason—a person might opine, from within this tradition—that body movement in the presence of music operates on the same model; namely, body movement must be *caused* by our perceptions of the music. On this view, music, rhythm (our perceptual experiences of these) cause us to move. Again, when the body's relationship with mental representations is conceived of as one of causes and effects, it will seem natural to understand certain body movements as *effects* of representations.

Merleau-Ponty: Motor intentionality

By exploring some of the ways in which Merleau-Ponty's nonrepresentational account of perception differs from the traditional view—with an emphasis upon body movement—we can elucidate the dominant aspect of groove, its feel, and at the same time clarify the role of the body in grooves. (Obviously, the reader should not expect a complete account of Merleau-Ponty's view of perception in what follows.)

Merleau-Ponty does not deny that we *can* represent things; he holds that representing is secondary and derivative. Our primary way of perceiving and acquiring knowledge of the world rests on our basic bodily engagement with things—our bodily capacities, dispositions, skills, and so on. In the section of his *Phenomenology of Perception* entitled, "The Spaciality of One's Own Body and Motricity," Merleau-Ponty puts the point in this way: "The motor experience of our body is not a particular case of knowledge; rather, it offers us a manner of reaching the world and the object, a 'praktognosia', that must be recognized as original, and perhaps as originary. My body has its world, or understands its world without having to go through 'representations' …"[24] We can attain an even clearer sense of this by considering Taylor Carman's description of Merleau-Ponty's view of embodied perception: "Perception is not mental representation, according to Merleau-Ponty, but skillful bodily orientation and negotiation in given circumstances. To perceive is not to have inner mental states, but to know and find your way around in an environment."[25] And further, Carman writes, "Perception and movement are not related to

one another as causes and effects, but coexist in a complex intercon-
nected whole."[26]

Other existential phenomenologists, who draw from Heidegger and
Merleau-Ponty, emphasize the active, bodily nature of perception as
well. Hubert Dreyfus's approach is instructive. Concerning Dreyfus's
view, the philosopher Joseph Rouse writes, "Not only does Dreyfus
follow Heidegger in seeing practical coping as a kind of revealing; he
explicitly denies any sharp contrast between acting and perceiving.
Perceiving is neither a passive registration nor an intellectual synthesis,
but is itself a kind of coping activity. Seeing a moving object, hearing
spoken words, tasting a liquid, or feeling a texture requires an appropriate bodily set and a coordinated exploratory movement."[27]

To get a bead on what Merleau-Ponty has in mind regarding body
movement and perception, and particularly to begin to think about
Merleau-Ponty's notion of motor intentionality, it helps to notice that
there are two sorts of body movement to which he is not referring.
First, some of our movements are cognitive engagements with our
environment. For example, if I ask a waiter at a restaurant for information about the size of a large Coke, he may think about it for a
split second, then hold his hands, palms facing, five inches apart,
indicating the height of the large glass. This is a reflective, cognitive
act. Second, contrast this cognitive behavior with an automatic reflex,
such as the movement of your foot when a doctor taps your knee. The
kind of movement Merleau-Ponty has in mind is, in a way, *between*
these other kinds of movement.[28]

The kinds of bodily capacities and skills Merleau-Ponty has in
mind are such as grasping/turning a door handle, grasping a can
of Coke, typing, and so on. Consider typing. The finger movements
involved are obviously not automatic reflexes, but they are also not
cognitive, reflective acts such as thinking about where a key is before
depressing it.[29] Importantly, such movements are *intentional* in the
phenomenologist's sense that they are *directed toward* their objects.

In these cases, it is our *bodies* not our thoughts that are directed toward things.[30] Merleau-Ponty refers to this category of bodily movements as "motor intentionality." In such practical behavior, we are *bodily* directed toward objects in our environment. In performing an action such as grasping a mug (a motor-intentional behavior) my body is directed toward the mug. In Merleau-Ponty's words,

> The gesture of reaching one's hand out toward an object contains a reference to the object, not as a representation, but as this highly determinate thing toward which we are thrown, next to which we are through anticipation, and which we haunt. Consciousness is being toward the thing through the intermediary of the body. A movement is learned when the body has understood it, that is, when it has incorporated it into its "world", and to move one's body is to aim at the things through it, or to allow one's body to respond to their solicitation, which is exerted upon the body without any representation. Motricity is thus not, as it were, a servant of consciousness, transporting the body to the point of space that we imagine beforehand.[31]

Regarding this aspect of Hubert Dreyfus's interpretation of Merleau-Ponty (and Heidegger), Joseph Rouse writes, "The intentionality of practical coping is a directedness of bodies rather than minds. Dreyfus emphasizes bodily coordination and orientation toward the task at hand, as one hammers a nail, sits in a chair, drives to the grocery, or exchanges pleasantries at a party. ... Bodies, one might say, are *geared* toward the world."[32] Notice the difference from an automatic, mechanical reflex; in a reflex movement, I am not directed toward anything.[33] Notice further that this motor-intentional understanding is not like the act of moving my hand and finger in order to point at a particular mug in order to answer a question about (say) which mug I received when I was hired at Montclair. That kind of body movement is reflective, cognitive.

As Hubert Dreyfus has emphasized (after being pressed a bit by John Searle), a motor-intentional act—which is, more or less, what

Dreyfus describes as "skillful coping"—is intentional not only insofar as it is directed at the world but also insofar as it can succeed or fail; it involves satisfaction conditions.[34] I may attempt to pick up a mug, and it may momentarily slip from my grip; I may momentarily fail to find a suitable distance for perceptually taking in a painting in an art gallery. In these cases, we fail to cope, fail to "deal with" things, fail to "manage" things.

Motor intentionality: Ground of cognition

According to Merleau-Ponty, our most basic apprehension of our environment, our grip on our situations, comes through such bodily dispositions, capacities, and skills. Merleau-Ponty writes, "Finally, these clarifications allow us to understand motricity unequivocally as original intentionality. Consciousness is originarily not an 'I think that' but rather an 'I can.'"[35] This comportment constitutes an embodied perspective; it gives us our experiential perspective on the world, our lived experience, what Merleau-Ponty calls the "phenomenal field." The phenomenal field is Merleau-Ponty's characterization of that which phenomenologists set out to describe.[36]

This embodied grip on the world is a basic comprehension; it grounds our more typically perceptual, as well as intellectual capacities. In fact, according to Merleau-Ponty, it is a precondition for cognitive understanding.[37] As Carman writes, concerning Merleau-Ponty,

All thought, all knowledge, all kinds of pictorial and linguistic representation—indeed, the very foregrounding of *objects* against background settings and situations—presuppose more basic modes of being-in-the-world, above all bodily situated perception. ... Merleau-Ponty's phenomenology is not a theory of mental representation, but a descriptive account of perception as a mode of being-in-the-world, an existential condition of the very possibility of representations—imaginative, semantic, or otherwise cognitive—intervening *between* ourselves and the world."[38]

To drive the point home, consider the philosopher Eric Matthews's words, "We can represent the world only because we are already present in it and involved with it."[39] I will claim below that this precognitive level at which our bodies situate us in our environments is the level at which we engage with (perceive, experience, understand) grooves—we do not primarily engage with grooves in terms of mental representations (as a traditional view would maintain).

3.5 Motor-intentional feel and movement

What is especially important about Merleau-Ponty's view for our purposes is that motor intentionality is *qualitative* in a special sense. As Carman writes, "We have—and know *and feel ourselves to have*—optimal bodily attitudes that afford us a 'best grip' on things, for example the right distance and angle from which to see something, a preferred posture in which to listen or concentrate, or to achieve poise and balance."[40] In other words, regarding perceptual situations or tasks, we experience bodily *feelings* of rightness and wrongness, a feel for perceptual orientation. On this issue, it is useful to quote Merleau-Ponty at length.

> For each object, just as for each painting in an art gallery, there is an optimal distance from which it asks to be seen—an orientation through which it presents more of itself—beneath or beyond which we merely have a confused perception due to excess or lack. Hence, we tend toward the maximum of visibility and we seek, just as when using a microscope, a better focus point, which is obtained through a certain equilibrium between the interior and the exterior horizons. ... The distance between me and the object is not a size that increases or decreases, but rather a

tension that oscillates around a norm. The oblique orientation of the object in relation to me is not measured by the angle that it forms with the plane of my face, but rather experienced as a disequilibrium, as an unequal distribution of its influences upon me.[41]

Consider this quotation by Taylor Carman regarding Merleau-Ponty's notion of motor-intentional feel. "The intentionality of perception thus depends crucially on the normativity of the body schema. The rightness and wrongness of perceptual appearances are interwoven with the felt rightness and wrongness of our bodily attitudes. We have a *feel* for the kinds of balance and posture that afford us a correct and proper view of the world."[42] Notice that this feeling of the body tensing-up when obtaining a less than optimal perceptual grip, and untensing as perceptual equilibrium is approached, constitutes a particular and unusual category of feelings. One thing these feelings do is to alert one's body to the rightness and wrongness of the body's position as regards a perceptual task. This particular set of feelings is thoroughly embodied. Such feelings do not merely provide one with an awareness of one's body's position and movement (which is the traditional way of conceiving of proprioception and kinesthesis); rather, motor-intentional feelings inform and direct the body's grasp of its environment, as well as, ultimately, knowledge acquisition. As Carman writes, "What allows our attitudes to be right or wrong about the world in the most basic way is the sense of bodily equilibrium that determines which postures and positions allow us to perceive things *properly*, and which constitute liabilities, incapacities, discomforts, and distortions."[43]

Understanding in movement

Our bodies do not merely serve to give us an *orientation* toward things, which then constitutes a foundation for subsequent, full-blown, cognitive understanding; our bodily engagement with things is *itself* a kind of understanding. Our bodily apprehension is a practical, prereflective, noncognitive sort of understanding. This is the kind of understanding that rests in our active engagement with objects. We often understand things we deal with t*hrough* our bodily actions.

For example, you may have a particular jacket that has an oddly placed top button or buttonhole. If you wear the jacket frequently, you come to understand how to manage the button and hole. But that know-how, that skill, is not reflective, not cognitive; rather, it is an understanding "in your fingers," so to speak. Importantly, this understanding is only activated as you are doing the buttoning. While your jacket is not present, if I ask you what the source of the problem is with your jacket—is the problematic button located a bit high or is the button hole a bit too small?—you may not be able to tell me. But you can negotiate the buttoning with your fingers, in the act. Along these lines, Merleau-Ponty considers the motor-intentional example of typing:

> One can know how to type without knowing how to indicate where on the keyboard the letters that compose the words are located. Knowing how to type, then, is not the same as knowing the location of each letter on the keyboard, nor even having acquired a conditioned reflex for each letter that is triggered upon seeing it. ... But if habit is neither a form of knowledge nor an automatic reflex, then what is it? It is a question of a knowledge in our hands, which is only given through a bodily effort and cannot be translated by an objective designation.[44]

In his "Edmund Husserl and Phenomenology," while contrasting certain of Merleau-Ponty's views with Husserl's, Sean Kelly considers the example of our embodied understanding of the features of a coffee mug—even the features that we do not see. Kelly writes, "The understanding of the entire object that I have when I am grasping it is not an understanding I can have independent of my bodily activity with respect to it. My bodily activity with respect to the object just is my way of understanding it."[45] Regarding another example, Kelly writes, "In motor-intentional activity, in other words, there is not an independent way that we have of understanding the object, on the basis of which we act differently with respect to it. Rather, our bodily activity is itself a kind of understanding of the object."[46]

Discussions of motor intentionality typically have to do with our engagement with space and spatial features; regarding examples such as grasping mugs, Kelly writes, "Grasping is the canonical motor-intentional activity."[47] Grooves obviously have to do with time rather than space. Temporal noncognitive understanding seems to me to be embodied no less than spatial understanding is embodied. Consider examples of practical understanding that are at least partially temporal, such as deciding when to step onto an escalator or deciding when to step into a revolving door. Consider a boxer's understanding of the speed bag or a runner's grasp of a treadmill. Consider the timing, the groove, of sex; this is not only a relevant example but an histori-cally important touchstone for rhythm and blues, rock and roll, and jazz grooves. In cases such as these, the knowledge we possess is not cognitive but in the body.

3.6 Wrap-up

In 3.1, I highlight some connections between music and the body. In 1993, Bruce Baugh claimed that rock music is essentially visceral, and that we must incorporate this into our aesthetic theory in order to correctly understand the art form. In response to Baugh, Stephen Davies contends that this visceral dimension is potentially present in experiences of all kinds of music, even classical music. Davies highlights the bodily ways in which we tend to react to music— tapping, swaying, and so on. Given this pervasive connection to the body, it is unsurprising that grooves are referred to with bodily metaphors, such as leaning and pushing. Davies explicitly characterizes this visceral dimension in terms of responses (effects, body movement) which the music causes. This is a common way of understanding the relationship between music and the body. For our purposes, however, this cause/effect relationship is not the interesting or illuminating relationship between music and the body.

We can learn something valuable about the relationships between music and the body by considering the different kinds of body movements of musicians, which I turn to in 3.2. First, musicians purposely move their fingers, hands, feet, lips, and so on, in order to give rise to some sound via their instrument. Clearly, this is not a response to the music. Second, some movements are not required to create the sound but serve as a technical aid. For example, to achieve a certain smoothness of rhythm, a drummer playing eighth notes on hi-hat cymbals might move her arm in a large motion with every other strike, while she plays the in-between notes with wrist movements alone. Third, musicians make the same kinds of movements Davies highlights—foot-tapping, finger-snapping, head swaying, and so on. This movement is not directly related to making music. Typically, these are movements to the music's pulse (in the cases we are considering, the pulse is the steady—1, 2, 3, 4—of the music). These movements are not merely effects caused by the music; tapping one's foot, swaying one's head, for example, are movements musicians perform. It is a commonplace for guitar teachers to tell their students to tap a foot, for instance, because it will help the student keep time or grasp a song's rhythm. I suggest that this sort of movement is not merely an aid to playing but helps a musician to hear, grasp a rhythm. One would expect it to do the same for listeners. If this is right, then we can see that there is a kind of body movement that listeners perform, purposively; some movements are not merely effects caused by the music.

In 3.3 I consider, again, the work of Vijay Iyer, both as a way of reinforcing the importance of the connection between the body and groove, and for the purpose of clearly distinguishing my approach and account from his. Iyer emphasizes the connections between the body and groove in a number of ways. For instance, he highlights the resonances between certain grooves and certain social behaviors, such as particular religious rituals. He notes the importance of the body in playing grooves. And further, he draws upon psychological research in order to argue that certain neural systems involved in rhythm and groove perception are also involved in body movement. I suggest that grounding his account on this last sort of point is a mistake in order to construct a truly active, embodied account of groove (as Iyer is aspiring to do), it must center on actual body movement.

According to the traditional, representational view of perception, perceiving is to have internal representations that are caused by external stimuli. On this view, as I discuss in 3.4, the role of the body in perception is explainable in terms of causes and effects—both in the sense that things in the world have effects on my body that result in representations, and instrumentally, in the sense that my mind causes my body to look to the left or to touch the keyboard. Under the umbrella of this view of perception, it is unsurprising that the relationship between music and body movement would be conceived in terms of cause and effect. From the perspective of this view, music, rhythm—our perceptual experiences of these—cause us to move.

Merleau-Ponty holds that representing is secondary and derivative; our primary way of perceiving and acquiring knowledge of the world rests on our bodily engagement, our ability to deal with objects, and to find our way around in our environments. In 3.4, I highlight Merleau-Ponty's notion of motor intentionality. Motor intentionality is "intentional" in so far as it involves being bodily *directed toward* things: examples include grasping and turning a door handle or handling a coffee mug. Merleau-Ponty maintains that this embodied grip on the world is a noncognitive way of knowing, and a precondition for cognitive understanding. Importantly, motor intentionality has an affective dimension (3.5). What is this motor-intentional feel? It is a kind of bodily feeling that informs our body's practical grasp of its environment. Merleau-Ponty's example of perceiving a painting in an art gallery is instructive. When I approach a painting, I find myself moving to the optimal distance for perceiving the painting; the adjustment is guided by a felt rightness or wrongness that leads me away from locations that are perceptually too far or too close, and inclines me toward the optimal distance. I also explore in 3.5 the notion that motor intentionality is not merely a way of perceiving but can also constitute an embodied sort of understanding. We come to understand, for example, the degree of slipperiness of an icy sidewalk by means of our bodily engagement with it. Or consider your understanding of a computer keyboard; it is not cognitive but it resides in your fingers. Your familiarity with the computer keyboard, your ability to *deal* with it, is activated in your motor-intentional activity. In the next chapter, we will apply these insights to the task of making sense of the feel and understanding of groove.

4

Groove in Music

4.1 Groove and the body

We have seen that musicians and music enthusiasts often talk as though understanding a groove has something to do with grasping the feel of the groove, and also that this comprehension has something principally to do with the body. In the last chapter, we laid the groundwork for conceiving of this embodied comprehension and feel in terms of Merleau-Ponty's account of perception, and especially his notion of motor intentionality. I have been working up to this: *What is the nature of the feel of grooves? The feel of a groove is the affective dimension of the relevant motor-intentional movements.* The feel of a groove is a motor-intentional feel.[1] The feel of a groove is not merely a quality of experience—not even some mixture of perceptual qualities of audition, proprioception, and so on; the feel of a groove is more integrally linked to the *understanding* of a groove than such a view would allow. The feel of a groove is a central element of the body's motor-intentional engagement with rhythmic elements of music.

We have seen that the feel is the dominant aspect of groove. The feel is a musician's datum. Our goal, however, is not merely to provide some hints as to how to effectively describe the experiences of the various feels of grooves. We want our elucidation of the feel we find at the center of the phenomenon of groove, in general, to be integrally linked to the way in which grooves are understood. Experiencing a groove's feel is necessary for understanding it. To put it another way, if a person understands everything about a particular groove only in analytical terms (in terms of the way in which the timing nuances deviate from the categorial time-values, and so on) she will not understand the groove. A person who does not experience the feel does not grasp the effect (the nonstructural objective, in the terminology of Chapter 1) which the drummer set out to achieve by performing the timing nuances. This listener also will not understand how the various elements of the rhythm hang together—nor the relations between the nuances and other instruments and voices. In some cases, not grasping the way in which the nuances relate to other aspects of the music makes it impossible to understand why a musician chooses to perform this or that nuance in the first place.

The experience of a groove is a necessarily active experience. We have seen that there is a noncognitive kind of understanding that is achieved *through* bodily activities (we understand how to type through certain movements; we know how to deal with a mug, a door handle, or a jacket's buttons, through the relevant motor-intentional movements). Similarly, we come to understand a groove *through* an activity of the body. The activity I have in mind is, at a minimum, moving some part of one's body to the music's pulse. This is the kind of movement musicians and listeners regularly display, which I discussed in Chapter 3: foot-tapping to the pulse, head-bobbing, swaying, finger-snapping, and so on. Notice that, on my view, the role of body movement is very different from the way these movements are often characterized, where a movement is considered to be an effect caused by the music.

We can begin to clarify this role of the body in groove experience and understanding by analogy to one of Merleau-Ponty's examples of motor intentionality. Recall his example of the body's movement in an art gallery, in the attempt to find the right distance to stand in order to optimally see a painting, discussed in Chapter 3: "The oblique orientation of the object in relation to me is not measured by the angle that it forms with the plane of my face, but rather experienced as a disequilibrium" (see 3.5).[2] Note that this example is different in an important way from the other motor-intentional examples I have mentioned, in that it involves a kind of *bodily exploration* through movement. In dealing with a door knob, once you've learned how to deal with a certain kind of door knob, the body doesn't engage in too many experimental movements; obtaining the proper bodily comportment is more or less immediate. Hubert Dreyfus has noticed this difference: "Paintings are interesting special cases in which we are still learning, so that we have to experiment with each painting, making trial and error movements that oscillate around the optimum, in order to find the best grip, whereas, in everyday experience, once we have learned to cope with a certain type of object, we are normally drawn directly to the optimal coping point."[3]

The body movement that seeks to "get" a groove is even more exploratory than the movement considered in the art gallery example above, because it is a repeated, rhythmic movement. With our bodies, we must explore the music by engaging in certain movements that open up the possibility of experiencing a groove's feel. Understanding a groove, coping with it, dealing with it, "getting" it, means to hear a performance's rhythm and timing nuances *as* pushes, its late notes *as* pulls, and so on. This is what it means to correctly grasp the performance's rhythm and timing nuances (the first aspect of groove) in an engaged manner, to possess what I am calling the facility for groove. Recall that this facility also involves being able to hit upon an adequate perceptual structure; it involves perceptual indeterminacy, and so on (see Chapter 2). It is to grasp how all of the parts fit together, *qualitatively*. When we perceive timing nuances in an analytical manner, we experience the nuances simply *as* off-time, simply *as* early or late. Notice that this latter way of hearing is, indeed, to comprehend something, namely, the nuances, and perhaps even the degree to which they are early or late. But it is to comprehend them in a manner that is detached from the dominant aspect of a groove, the feel. Hearing the eighth notes merely as off-time is to fail to grasp the coherence of the elements of a groove, which can involve multiple rhythmic elements created by any number of instruments.

Body movement is exploratory in engaging with a groove because it is rarely obvious on a first hearing precisely how to move, and precisely how to listen, so as to make sense of how all the rhythmic elements cohere. This is especially difficult in listening to genres with which one is unfamiliar (I will consider this in more detail below). At first, some rhythmic elements may seem simply to be outliers. The comprehension of the coherence comes through finding the right, repetitive movement, the effective targets of attention, the right perceptual structure, and so on. We have seen, for example (in Chapter 2), that certain elements of a groove are best heard as in the background. The conditions for this aesthetic experience are set by a particular bodily comportment; in other words, certain features of the music recede into the background, naturally, depending upon how one moves. We are now beginning to see the ways in which the earlier considerations about perceptual structure are related to body movement.

We can see that bodily movement to a rhythm, to a pulse, is not merely a reaction to a rhythm (movement is not merely caused by the music). Body movement is not merely a sympathetic reaction to a rhythm. Another way to put the point I mentioned just above is that the movement aids a listener in establishing a perceptual structure conducive to experiencing a groove.[4] When one grasps a groove, the timing variations show up in experience as motor-intentional tensions against a norm; the norm is the rhythm's pulse; the tensions are provided by the timing nuances.[5] "Getting" a groove, "grooving," or "being in the groove" means that one possesses a noncognitive, felt, bodily grasp of a performance's or a recording's pulse, rhythmic pattern, and various timing nuances (and although I have not been emphasizing this, I have mentioned that dynamics, timbre, and tempo shifts are also involved).

Aesthetic experience

There are, of course, ways in which the noncognitive, bodily under-standing of a groove is unlike most bodily *skills*, such as typing, hammering, and so on. In an important sense: "getting" a groove is not an ordinary example of know-how or coping *because it is an aesthetic experience*. What is an aesthetic experience? There are many accounts of aesthetic experience; John Dewey's and Monroe Beardsley's are noteworthy.[6] For our purposes, we can rest with the most uncontroversial, defining feature of aesthetic experience; namely, aesthetic experiences possess qualities that we take to be worthy of attention in themselves. Unlike typing or grasping a mug, comprehending a groove places on a pedestal the affective dimension of motor intentionality. We have certainly seen that those who engage with grooves emphasize the feel of grooves. In coming to understand a groove, the guiding, affective dimension of motor intentionality is not secondary to the task at hand.

In the nonaesthetic cases, the motor-intentional feel does not seem to be entirely unconscious: the feel informs skilled behavior. In the case of groove, the feel similarly informs our embodied way of grasping specific timing in a context—but importantly, the feel is also the dominant, unifying quality of the aesthetic experience.[7] Notice that, regarding the nonaesthetic examples, our attention is typically directed toward the purpose of the task at hand, rather than whatever qualities may be riding in the background, informing the skilled activity or coping. Consider typing, shooting free throws in basketball, grasping a door handle, and so on. In all of these examples, we typically attend to the objective of the action rather than any bodily feelings that may, in the background, inform that action.[8]

As we have seen, the affective tension, equilibrium, and so on, which informs the relevant motor-intentionality activity is the feel of a groove. This feel is the dominant aspect of the phenomenon of groove. Again, in the case of groove, *bodily feelings* that typically merely *guide* us in dealing practically with things in our environment—to take temporal examples: guiding you in entering a busy freeway from an entrance ramp, guiding you regarding when you can step onto an escalator, etc.—become qualities worthy of attention as ends in themselves, if the groove is interesting. We bask in a groove's motor-intentional feel while moving our bodies to the rhythms.

The noncognitive grasping of a groove by moving to the pulse, and the feel that informs this motor-intentional activity, are two sides of the same coin: to "get" a groove just is to comprehend it bodily and to feel that comprehension.

A critic of my view may object that it seems far-fetched to claim that body movement is *required* to comprehend a groove. My first response to such a criticism is to lean on a Merleau-Pontean, existential phenomenological view of perception in general. Recall Joseph Rouse's comments about Hubert Dreyfus's view: "Not only does Dreyfus follow Heidegger in seeing practical coping as a kind of revealing; he explicitly denies any sharp contrast between acting and perceiving. Perceiving is neither a passive registration nor an intellectual synthesis, but is itself a kind of coping activity. Seeing a moving object, hearing spoken words, tasting a liquid, or feeling a texture requires an appropriate bodily set and a coordinated exploratory movement."[9] Further, notice that my view explains a lot. For example, it gives us a way of understanding why it is that the feel of a groove has a bodily character (we need that clarity to make sense of the bodily metaphors, such as leaning, pushing, and so on). My view also provides a way of understanding (via motor intentionality) the way in which body movement is integrally connected to the feel of a groove and to the understanding of it. Also, if my critic agrees that we need a way of making sense of how we understand grooves, which does not reduce to mere listening, and is also not an intellectual sort of understanding, I have provided that. Here is an additional, empirical point. Recall Stephen Davies's observation that, in our encounters with music, visceral responses are even more prevalent than we realize. He claims that we move our bodies in the presence of music, sometimes even when we are unaware of moving: "Music's regularities and its cross-patterns are echoed kinesthetically by both the performer and the listener, who twitch, tap, contract, flex, twist, jerk, tense, sway, and stretch as they react bodily to the music. Music moves us, quite literally, and often we are unaware of the small motions we make in response to it."[10] Unlike Davies, I do not interpret this pervasive movement in the presence of music as evidence that music *causes* us to move. I take it at face value: where there is music, there is movement. Davies's observation of pervasive movement lends some small amount of support to my view: I would say to my critic: we do not frequently observe listeners *not* moving; the movement is there, we are just disagreeing about how to interpret it."

Affective and movement details

The felt quality of a groove is a motor-intentional feel: a feel that informs our body movements as we attempt to cope with a rhythm and its elements. Nevertheless, perhaps we can say more about this feel by *describing* this affective element of a few different kinds of grooves. Movement to a pulse has the effect of emphasizing, experientially, the pulse. Insofar as a pulse is regular, bodily expectations are established. Certain musical elements fail to meet these expectations (the early/late eighth notes), and so they seem to pull or push against the expected regular timing. When we are moving to the pulse, we feel these satisfied or thwarted expectations in our bodies. While moving to a pulse, late eighth notes are experienced—not as late to a specific degree, not as so many instances of an "eighth note(-4)"—but as pulling against the regularity of the movement of one's body. In other words, through movement to the pulse, I set up expectations of rhythmic regularity in my body. Timing nuances thwart that regularity, and these tensions are felt more profoundly than many other perceptual qualities because they are felt in and by the body as a bodily disequilibrium.

In considering the feel of groove, we have focused on the tensions—pushes, pulls, and so on. But grooves can also feel buoyant. The percussionist, author, and ethnomusicologist, John Miller Chernoff, has said, "[Groove] also suggests coolness and calm, something effortless and smooth, as in 'groovin'. In its physical aspect, it keeps you with it, 'in the groove.'"[11] We can make sense of this by considering a drummer's perspective. While a drummer is creating a groove, after the equilibrium brought on by the regularity of the initial pulse is thwarted by the pull of late eighth notes (say), he works to achieve a new equilibrium, one in which the pulling recurs regularly enough so that the pulling feels less like a destructive force and more like a new position (a leaning backward). The pulls then show up in the new equilibrium as interesting, felt complexities. Now, breaking-up the initial equilibrium took some effort, as did establishing the new one. Aided by his body movement, the drummer had to work to find the right time-values (as well as accents, timbres, and so on) for creating this groove. But once the groove is constituted, the drummer's task becomes easier; like driving a car in snow-grooves, he feels that there is some external force—in the music—guiding his movements and limbs. It is in this feeling of being guided that he feels as though he has been pulled in to a musical notch. And the consequence of the musical notch is the easing of his task; this is the cradle of buoyancy. A good example of this is Ringo Starr's performance on "All My Lovin.'"[12] As a result of being aided by this force in the music, the drummer is able to redirect his energy and concentration to more subtle aspects of playing, and so to lift his performance to higher levels. For listeners as well as players, the buoyancy of a groove is the result of the felt support that comes from finding equilibrium in repetition, even if it is built upon tense pulls and pushes. Even a groove that has a disjointed feel repeats, and when it does, we grow accustomed to it. As we get used to it, the feel becomes uplifting and invigorating.

I recall seeing a particular NBA basketball playoff game in which Michael Jordan made several amazing shots. One shot, late in the game, was a seemingly impossible, long, three-point shot. He made the shot while literally falling down. Just afterward, jogging up the court, he turned toward his teammates on the bench, and to the sportscasters, and shrugged his shoulders—as if to admit that he had no idea how he did it. As a drummer, with a groove "under you," so to speak, supporting you, you feel emboldened to try things that you would ordinarily not try. The complex notes of difficult drum fills effortlessly fall in with the time-values and accent structure laid down by the groove. This is the buoyant feeling, the sense in which a groove is like an athlete's "zone." Engaged listeners share in this sense of buoyancy.

Some grooves may involve, primarily, one set of repeating nuances. We have discussed this sort for simplicity's sake. In such a case, perceiving those nuances engagedly is to experience a certain pull (say), which just is the feel of the groove. But consider a groove that is more complex, such as the groove of Sly and The Family Stone's 1969 recording, "Thank You (Falettinme Be Mice Elf Agin)."[13] In the introduction alone, there are many timing nuances present in the rhythm guitar and the bass guitar. The feel of such grooves is, of course, not identical to the engaged perception of one repeating nuance. The feel is multifarious. The feel of this groove is, let's say, snake-like: it moves and shifts, with pulls and pushes being generated by multiple instruments. The point I want to emphasize is that, regarding more complex grooves, the nonstructural objective of one set of nuances (a pull, push, etc.) will constitute only one part of the recording's or the performance's groove. The groove itself will consist of a combination of these elements.

4.2 Movement styles

Some of the intuitions underlying Richard Shusterman's theory of somaesthetics resonate with my project. Like Bruce Baugh (see 3.1), but regarding aesthetics in general, Shusterman believes that core thinkers in the tradition of aesthetics are mistaken for failing to conceive of aesthetic appreciation, judgment, and so on, as having to do with the body. Some of the points Shusterman makes jibe with the general direction of my view. For example, in his *Performing Live: Aesthetic Alternatives for the Ends of Art*, he writes, "Rock and roll songs are typically enjoyed through moving, dancing, and singing along with the music …"[14] But then, on the same page, he signals that he is referring to body movement as an effect: "The more energetic and kinesthetic aesthetic *response evoked* by rock music exposes the fundamental passivity of the traditional aesthetic attitude of disinterested, distanced contemplation …"[15] For such reasons, I have not conceived of my project through Shusterman's theory. But here, I want to focus on one of Shusterman's insights that can help us to steer clear of a potential mistake. Although Shusterman does not consider Merleau-Ponty as much as one might expect in his writing, he emphasizes an important difference between his somaesthetics and Merleau-Ponty's views of the body:

> Rather than seeking to reveal an alleged primordial, foundational, universal embodied consciousness that (in Merleau-Ponty's words) is "unchanging, given once and for all" and "known by all men" in all cultures and times, I claim that somatic consciousness is always shaped by culture and thus admits of different forms in different cultures (or in different subject positions within the same culture).[16]

Setting aside whether this is a viable criticism of Merleau-Ponty, Shusterman's point is a good one, and we should consider it. Surely, in different cultures we find different rhythms and grooves as well as different styles of body movement. Even within one city in the USA (say, Minneapolis) one can hear different grooves and see different styles of body movement. Even within one music venue on the same night (First Avenue, for instance), one can hear different grooves and see different styles of body movement. I do not pretend to be a nuanced observer of the differences between people or their styles of movement, but here are a few basic observations that are easy to make. Punk audiences (especially those of the late 1970s and early 1980s) threw their bodies into one another, often while jumping up and down repeatedly. This movement is not unlike the disjointed, fast rhythms and grooves of punk music. Heavy metal audiences swing their heads repeatedly forward and back, which resonates with the emphasized quarter notes of the rhythms (consider AC/DC's quarter-note emphasis). Funk audiences of the 1970s and 1980s often display more fine-grained, articulate movements in the body, which are similar to the complex accent structures and nuances of the rhythms and grooves. One could make similar observations about the differences among techno audiences, jazz audiences, hip-hop audiences, country music audiences, and so on. The bottom line is that we see different kinds of movement, different styles of movement, in different cultural groups, as well as different groups of people immersed in one genre of music or another. Some of these movements are unique to (or emphasized at) performances but others are observable even in private listening.

The point I want to stress is that, in claiming that one must move in order to grasp a groove, I certainly do not mean to suggest that there is only one kind of movement, or one style of movement, which everyone must perform in order to grasp every kind of groove. While the view I have set out provides an underlying and general way of understanding the relationships between movement, grasping grooves, and their feels (in terms of motor intentionality), this is consistent with the fact that different individuals have different styles of movement. There are obviously differences between cultures in general, and even more finely, between musical cultures. As Vijay Iyer correctly observes—and this is his main point about *situated* cognition—"Although every music listener has a body … every culture 'constructs' the human body differently."[17]

An older source from which to extract this basic point is the work of the sociologist-philosopher Pierre Bourdieu. One can extract this point by highlighting the class variability of what Pierre Bourdieu calls the "aesthetic habitus."[18] Bourdieu's habitus is a system of dispositions acquired through one's experience in a social context. Merleau-Ponty's direct influence upon Bourdieu is manifest in Bourdieu's characterization of the habitus as "techniques of the body" or "embodied schemes."[19] The "aesthetic habitus" is what Bourdieu calls the aptitude for perceiving and understanding art in *traditional* terms: artworks are autonomous objects which can only be recognized as such through disinterested perception, emphasizing form over extra-artistic function and over content (this description emerges largely from Bourdieu's interpretation of Immanuel Kant). Bourdieu argues that philosophers have been mistaken insofar as they base universal, ahistorical claims about (say) aesthetic judgment upon a historically contingent attitude.[20] This traditional, Kantian view is the one Shusterman and Baugh criticize.

Bourdieu stops short of making an important point that Shusterman makes in a criticism of Bourdieu.[21] Shusterman laments the fact that Bourdieu did not allow for an *alternative* aesthetic. Bourdieu contrasts the dominant aesthetic with the working-class aesthetic. The working-class, "popular aesthetic" is one that emphasizes content over form; the working classes prefer artworks on the basis of the real-world values depicted. Here is the point with which Shusterman, rightly, takes issue: according to Bourdieu, this popular aesthetic is not a true aesthetic. (It is noteworthy that Baugh's intuitions pulled him toward a similar conclusion, without, I assume, being aware of Bourdieu's work of undermining the traditional aesthetic.) The claim I want to rest with is this: even though different listeners have different, let's say, *movement profiles*, we can best understand the role of movement vis-à-vis groove (as well as best understand groove itself) in terms of motor intentionality.

4.3 Entrainment

Once we acknowledge this variability of movement profiles, along with the underlying importance of motor intentionality, it highlights a practically efficacious aspect of my view. I will lead up to this practical aspect of my view by way of a consideration of Vijay Iyer's work one last time, as well as a consideration of what some other theorists have had to say about entrainment.

Perhaps Iyer comes closest to a true, embodied view while discussing entrainment. Generally speaking, entrainment is the synchronization of two different rhythmic processes. In their *In Time With The Music: The concept of entrainment and its significance for ethnomusicology*, Martin Clayton and his collaborators write, "Entrainment describes a process whereby two rhythmic processes interact with each other in such a way that they adjust towards and eventually 'lock in' to a common phase and/or periodicity."[22] Although examining his thesis of musical meter[23] would take us too far afield, it is useful to consider what the music theorist Justin London says about entrainment in his *Hearing in Time: Psychological Aspects of Musical Meter*.[24] London's comments about entrainment rest upon an active conception of perceptual attention. He draws upon the work of the psychologist Mari Riess Jones, who writes, "Attending is an energistic activity guided in part by explicitly dynamic schemes that are themselves set in motion or indeed synchronously driven by the ongoing temporal character of an environment."[25] Regarding this process of synchronization (entrainment), Jones writes, "The interaction of the perceiver with moving world patterns is described by the principle of synchronization. Successive event onsets in world patterns simultaneously define a series of nested time periods, and corresponding to each world time period there is a synchronized perceptual rhythm with a similar period."[26]

The synchronization at issue is between music and brain processes. This is important for my purposes insofar as my view centers on body movement and motor intentionality. Later in London's book he draws upon the work of the psychologist Edward W. Large, who writes, "The basic idea is that when a network of neural oscillators, spanning a range of natural frequencies, is stimulated with a musical rhythm, a multi-frequency pattern of oscillations is established."[27] Although London ultimately claims that meter is "a kind of sensorimotor entrainment,"[28] his meaning of "motor" here, like Iyer's use, is very different from the view I have developed.

One central sense in which London's and Iyer's views can be described as sensori-*motor* or embodied, is that, for them, rhythm perception involves neural mechanisms that *have to do with body movement*—actual body movement is not a necessary component. Recall the statement by Todd quoted in Iyer (London also draws upon Todd): "[I]f the spatiotemporal form of certain [sensory] stimuli are matched to the dynamics of the motor system, then they may evoke a motion of an internal representation, or motor image, of the corresponding synergetic elements of the musculoskeletal system, *even if the musculoskeletal system itself does not move.*"[29] Along these lines, London writes, "The visceral sense of time and movement that beat perception engenders may be due to the strong links between rhythm perception and motor behavior; the tactus rate is the time frame that best affords our own rate of motion. To put it more plainly, to hear a beat is to sense *the potential for (if not actual) movement.*"[30] There are many other places in London's book and in Iyer's work where one can find references to mental "representations," as well as statements that indicate an emphasis upon brain activity (rather than body movement) such as this statement from London: "More plainly, meter is an aspect of what goes on *in your brain* while the music is playing."[31]

Occasionally, Iyer and London consider the entrainment of actual body movement, such as tapping one's foot to a rhythm.[32] When this is raised, they are usually discussing playing music. But even in cases where there is a discussion of tapping while listening, the tapping is conceived as *caused* by the music or the *neural events* that are synchronized to the music. The tapping is not conceived as integrally involved in an act of perceiving or comprehending itself, as my view has it. For example, Iyer refers to body movement as "induced":

> One often speaks of a musical groove as something that *induces* motion. In describing his aesthetic criteria for rhythm tracks, a colleague involved in hip-hop music distinguished between a musical excerpt that '*makes me* bob my head' and one that doesn't.[33] Many of us have witnessed motion *induced* in infants or toddlers via music, but this behavior is not universal, involuntary, or even reliable. This capacity to entrain to a regular aural pulse may be an evolutionary vestige of a previously useful ability that has more recently fallen into disuse. In any case, this phenomenon clearly involves regular, rhythmic bodily movement as a kind of sympathetic *reaction* to regular rhythmic sound—that is, as a kind of dance.[34]

Insofar as *sympathy* involves a give and take, this last sentence gestures in the direction of a true, embodied view. But if we are to make sense of what Iyer means by "sympathetic" in light of everything else he says, we must construe the movement as caused by neural processes that are entrained to the music. This is to miss the most important sense, as we have seen, in which groove perception and understanding are active and embodied.

I do not mean to dispute the relevance of some kind of synchronization capacity to perceiving rhythm and grooves, which, of course has something to do with neural activity. In my view, there may be some kinds of synchronization occurring between perceivers and the music, but it grows out of a bodily perception that involves motor intentionality. My problems with discussions of entrainment are that they seem to have to do with either a view of perception as mental representation, body movement as a mere effect of brain states, or both. Moreover, the relationship between body movement and music should not be construed as automatic in any way, which discussions of entrainment occasionally suggest. Clayton and his colleagues, for example, characterize entrainment as being locked in to a stimulus. Rather, we should emphasize that groove perception is exploratory, as I have suggested. This sets the stage for the practical point I have been leading up to.

4.4 A practical suggestion

As listeners, there are very concrete ways we can use body movement, in an exploratory manner, in attempts to grasp grooves with which we are not already familiar. Different listeners are, obviously, familiar with different kinds of music. Certain styles of music are more closely related than others. Someone familiar with the grooves of 1970s funk music will have an easier time grasping the grooves of hip-hop than will someone familiar only with country music, for instance.

Consider an interesting and unusual groove created by the timing nuances of a rapper's performance; take Eminem's rap on Dr. Dre's "Forgot about Dre."[35] A country music aficionado, who is unfamiliar with rap, may not immediately grasp Eminem's groove; she will not easily grasp why the timing of that rap is special. My practical suggestion for the country listener is to observe how hip-hop listeners move their bodies while listening to the genre, or better, to that particular track. I don't claim that there is only one way to move that "unlocks" a given groove, but there will be certain movements, or a certain style of movement, that will help. I have mentioned the sort of thing I have in mind above, regarding punk, heavy metal, and so on.

In the repeating portion of Eminem's rap—which begins, "Nowadays everybody wanna talk like they got something to say …"—he falls off the beat (deliberately, of course) in a couple of different ways. The words that involve timing nuances are, first, "… like they got something to say," and even more so, "… the mother-fuckers act like they forgot about Dre." To the uninitiated, these may sound simply like timing mistakes. If you move your body in a way that captures and tracks the background rhythm, which is quite jerky and abrupt, you slowly begin to hear the portions of Eminem's rap that fall off the beat (the timing nuances) *as* generators of tension and anticipation, which cause the entire groove to pull in a direction that I can only describe as sideways. I am not suggesting that a *particular* movement is a necessary or sufficient condition for hearing that groove. *Some* movement is necessary, but there will be a variety of movements that suffice. Regarding sufficiency, of course, there are other things one must accomplish in order to hear a groove. For example, in Chapter 2, I emphasized that one must allow certain musical elements to recede into the perceptual background, to remain ambiguous in perception, indeterminate, in Merleau-Ponty's sense (I argued above that these two sorts of conditions are related).

Some hip-hop and electronica rhythms are even more of a challenge to grasp, perhaps even for those who are familiar with related genres, such as funk. There is an extreme and artificial quality to some of these grooves, due to the way they are created. Hip-hop producers, such as Timbaland, or so-called IDM artists (Intelligent

Dance Music), such as Aphex Twin or Matmos, create innovative
rhythms on computers by turning off program tools that normalize
time-values. (These program tools, such as "quantization," automati-
cally move notes to the nearest selected time-value, e.g. a sixteenth
note.) By ear, then, these artists "paint" rhythms, often in short time-
loops, by manually moving the notes on the computer screen, or by
using keyboard interfaces, and then by listening to the results, in
loops, as they go. Some of these rhythms involve nuances that stretch
far beyond the boundaries of an ordinary drummer's pushing and
pulling (although, interestingly, contemporary drummers seem to
be evolving to be able to groove in these extreme ways). You might
listen to such a beat several times, and it may continue to sound
like complete chaos. A perfect example of this is the song "What
About Us?" by Brandy.[36] If there is a way for a person faced with this
seeming chaos to discover the underlying coherence of the groove,
I want to suggest that it is through attempting different kinds of
body movement while listening. There is another way to express
what we have been considering, which emphasizes the connections
between the issues examined in earlier and later chapters. When
you move your body to a pulse, or some other aspect of a rhythm, it
fosters a perceptual structure that de-emphasizes the specific time-
values of the nuances; this movement can set in relief the *relations*
between the elements. You will begin to discover a push or a pull
(an engaged perception of a nuance) where previously you heard
only an arbitrary or off-time note (an analytical perception of the
nuance). The movement draws into the pulse's wake elements that
you previously heard as chaotic, out of sync, or just plain wrong. You
now hear the chaotic elements as having fallen into place within the
pervasive pushing or pulling quality. And again, the push or the pull
(the groove) is the musicians' intended effect, which you had to work
to hear accurately, to comprehend.

4.5 Groove *in* music: Ontology

Now that we have our account of groove on the table, we should ask—what role do grooves occupy in music? That is, how do grooves factor in to what we understand music to be, and how do grooves factor in to the ways in which we evaluate music? By considering certain issues in musical ontology, we can make some illuminating observations. I will argue that grooves are central ingredients to certain genres of music. I will even suggest that there is something very like groove in classical performances, and perhaps even in classical musical works.

Musical ontologists ask what kind of thing a musical work is, what kind of entity. This question is not as odd as it may sound to the uninitiated, because we want to know exactly what it is that we are talking about when we describe and evaluate a work of music. What is the target of evaluation of Beethoven's Fifth Symphony? What is the target of evaluation of Brandy's "What About Us?" What is the (so to speak) primary text? In this regard, notice that music seems intuitively different from some other art forms, such as visual art. A traditional view of visual art ontology is that a painted work of art is simply the object hanging on the wall (say) in a museum—the painted canvas.[37] What is the musical work of art?

Classical music

In traditional philosophy of music, where the emphasis has been on classical music, a distinction is drawn between musical works and performances. Works are typically characterized in terms of musical structure, which is, more or less, represented in music notation, in the score. In the classical tradition, when someone describes or judges a musical work, she is typically referring to that structure. Other musical qualities are attributable to the performance.[38] Diana Raffman, whom we considered at length in the first chapters, adopts these traditional ontological assumptions. According to Raffman, musical nuances are properties of performances, contributing to a classical musician's style or his interpretation of a musical work. Consider this passage from her book:

> Robison's C-sharps may be slightly lower than Dwyer's, or Steinhardt's D-sharps a shade higher than his E-flats; DuPré may narrow her vibrato in tense passages and widen it in relaxed ones, while Rampal's E-naturals tend to be slightly flat in the middle register. These fine-grained details of a performance—these *nuances*—are features the score does not (indeed *cannot*) dictate, hence precisely the sorts of features the performer can manipulate in forging his peculiar interpretation of a musical work.[39]

Even concerning classical music, this standard ontology seems too austere. Consider the following more inclusive ontological view: a score does not exhaustively individuate the work; in addition to the represented structure, the work includes properties not represented in the score, properties that a composer assumes due to a given performance tradition and conventions of notation, which are part and parcel of the composer's musical milieu.[40] As Stephen Davies writes, "Not everything recorded in the score has the force of a work-determinative instruction, and some essential elements not registered in the score are implicit in the performance practice."[41] Moreover, "Not all the definitive features of the work are indicated in its score ... The instructions issued by scores are interpreted with respect to both the performance practices against which they are written and the notational conventions of the composer's day."[42] Davies offers the following examples:

> In the Viennese waltz, the second beat should sound a little earlier than the notation suggests. ... In the case of a piece composed in the early eighteenth century, the melody line should be decorated in repeats, vibrato should be used sparingly, and rhythms marked as "dotted" in the score should be played as if they are double-dotted. If

the piece is a Sarabande, the stress normally falls on the second beat of the bar, not the first. In a late-nineteenth-century classical piece, some string vibrato is required. The established conventions of the style or genre determine the "default" condition, so no sign of what is expected is needed in the score.[43]

For our purposes, what is interesting about this ontological view is that it conceives of musical nuances as more than merely properties of performances—even in classical music. Through performance traditions and notational conventions, what may appear to be merely characteristics of a performance can be seen instead to be features of the musical work itself. That is, some performance practices involve nuances; consequently, a musical work's essential properties might include a musical nuance through the assumptions of the performance practice. But are there classical grooves?

In *The Imaginary Museum of Musical Works*, the philosopher Lydia Goehr shows—among many other things—that an accurate musical ontology must be sensitive to the facts and norms of a musical practice.[44] To approach this cautiously, looking back at the tradition of classical music, of course, we do not find classical composers using the term "groove." However, if classical works of music involve timing nuances, those timing nuances have nonstructual, qualitative effects. By the same reasoning set out in earlier chapters, these effects are dominant (the effects are what a musician attends to in determining whether she has performed the nuances as intended). Drawing upon Davies's discussion, consider the Viennese waltz. What is the qualitative effect of playing the second beat a bit earlier than the notation indicates? Perhaps the effect can be described as a leaning-forward, a pushing, a feeling of urgency. However described, perceiving this quality correctly will require some active, perceptual work (it will involve achieving a particular perceptual structure). Flying in the face of traditional norms of stillness in the concert hall, I will venture a guess that that perceptual work will involve some body movement that can be elucidated in terms of motor intentionality (recall Davies's point, considered in Chapter 3, that "visceral responses" are ubiquitous in encounters with even classical music). If this is right, while these effects of timing nuances may not be literally conceived of as "grooves" in the classical tradition, I expect that there are *pushings, leanings, pullings*, and so on. While these effects of timing nuances are not as central to the classical tradition as they are to rock, hip-hop, and jazz, they are there. And if the ontology we have considered is correct, the nuances are features of the work (contra Raffman). What about the qualitative effects? Are the qualitative effects of these timing nuances features of the classical work or the performance? Regarding classical music, I leave that question for others to consider, although some of what I say below may suggest an answer.

Set aside the qualitative effects of nuances in the classical tradition. Consider some limitations on the inclusion of nuances themselves in classical works. *Specific* nuances cannot be essential properties of classical works (Raffman would certainly agree), whereas nuance *types* may be. Consider Davies's Viennese waltz observation above. The observation that supports my claim is that although a performance practice or notational convention might require that a note be slightly high or slightly early, it cannot require a *particular* degree of earliness, and so on. The same specificity limitation holds regarding other nuances. The classical composer might have an expressive variation *type* in mind, and that type might have an effect upon her choices, but *particular* nuances will not. For example, a classical composer may choose a given rhythmic pattern for a cello, involving nuances, but the classical composer will not have a specific degree of earliness in mind, which, if not performable (let's say), would cause her to choose a different rhythmic pattern. She may make a compositional decision based upon a nuance type (slightly early, perhaps) but she will not make a compositional decision based upon a specific nuance.[45] These limits are ultimately due to our limited abilities to remember and re-identify time-values, pitches, etc., as Raffman emphasizes.

Contemporary popular music

What sets apart rock, hip-hop, and pop from classical? Consider Theodore Gracyk's category of rock music (which is quite broad). In rock, nuances are among the principal objects of appreciation—it is structure that takes a back seat. As Gracyk notes, regarding rock, "song structure is often an incidental framing device for something further; a 'coathanger' ... upon which other qualities ... are hung."[46] And further, "Rock is a music of very specific sound qualities and their textural combination. Specific sounds are as central to the music as are specific colors in painting."[47] We should take "specific sounds qualities" to include pitch and timing nuances, as well as subtleties of timbre, dynamics, and so on. Gracyk is highlighting, among other things, the degree to which rock musicians concern themselves with the details of recording: "with modern recording technology, recording artists have as much control over the resulting sound as a visual artist over a print or painting."[48] Thus, while a score seems to capture (at least) a significant amount of what is salient about a classical work, it does not capture as much of what is salient about a work in rock music.

This emphasis upon nuances informs Gracyk's ontology of rock. Although rock music has stylistic roots in African-American music, according to Gracyk, rock is not defined in terms of musical style but in terms of its being centered on recording technology: "rock is a tradition of popular music whose creation and dissemination centers on recording technology."[49] As composers, rock musicians "compose ... with sound, not in notation."[50] The medium of the recording allows for the emphasis of fine-grained sound qualities, nuances. The rock musical work, according to Gracyk, *just is* the recording.

The recording is the primary text, the principal object of evaluation and criticism. And of course, if the recording is the work, nuances are essential properties of the work. As Stephen Davies writes regarding Gracyk's ontology, "If the primary works in rock are recordings, then these works are very thick with properties. Every aspect of the sound captured by the recording technology is constitutive of the work."[51]

When we survey the musical practices of contemporary styles such as rock, hip-hop, pop, and so on, we find grooves featured as central elements. An adequate ontology will have to reflect this. One way to note this emphasis is to consider the creative process. Particular grooves and particular nuances of timbre and pitch (among others) all may serve as criteria that rock musicians (broadly construed to include hip-hop, etc.) consider in the creative process. For instance, a rock composer may envision not merely a certain rhythm (which is a matter of structure) but a certain groove. She might imagine a rhythm that feels as though it pulls against the guitars to a very specific degree. If, upon trying to create this groove with her band, she discovers that the pulling between the drums and guitars cannot be achieved to her satisfaction, the composer may opt for a different rhythm altogether. In such a case, the groove is a central criterion in making compositional decisions, a central feature of the rock musical work—not merely a feature of the performance of it. The point to emphasize is that, in some situations, a subtle quality such as a groove can be more important to a composer than a structural feature such as a rhythmic pattern. This is a fact of the musical practice that ontology must reflect.

Another way to make these points is to say that, when one grasps a groove, it renders intelligible features of the work that were previously unintelligible (note how crucial this is for correctly evaluating such music). For example, the *reason* a composer chooses one rhythmic pattern over another may be unintelligible unless one grasps the groove that is possible through the chosen rhythmic pattern. Why are certain timing nuances performed in a song's verse but not the chorus? Such questions can be answered once one grasps the groove and the role of the nuances at issue in generating it. Why is the bass guitar playing a bit behind the drums? Why is the bass guitar playing such a simple part? (Regarding the latter, consider the simple bass pattern on recordings such as the Bo-Diddley-inspired "Willie and the Hand Jive," by the Johnny Otis Show.[52]) An understanding of the groove will reveal the reason, by making it clear just how that ingredient or slight variation contributes to the groove. Here is a question many drummers and record producers concern themselves with: why are audience members particularly drawn to engage with certain styles of music, or certain songs, by dancing? Do listeners dance to a particular song performed with one rhythmic pattern whereas they do not dance to the same song performed with a rhythmic pattern that is very similar? The answers will lie in the groove the musicians are able to ground.

I use the term "ground," as a way of transitioning to a suggestion for expanding upon Gracyk's rock ontology. We have seen that a groove is not merely a matter of what musicians do. A groove is not merely a certain collection of nuanced sounds performed by musicians live or occurring on a recording. We might say that, ontologically, a groove is *a phenomenon of experience*. A groove emerges, between musicians and listeners, when music is engaged with in a certain way. (By now, you know the way: it involves perceiving certain properties indeterminately, moving one's body to the pulse, and so on.) If I am right that grooves are features of these musical works, then an ontology of rock (including hip-hop, pop, etc.) must include not only the nuances but the effects of nuances, which as we have seen, require active work on the part of the perceiver.

In order to flesh out my ontological suggestion, I want to briefly consider Roman Ingarden's ontology of literature (I consider his ontology of literature rather than his ontology of music because the latter lacks a feature I want to develop). In his *The Literary Work of Art*,[53] Roman Ingarden argues that the literary work of art (LWA) is an intentional object. Roman Ingarden is a phenomenologist in the Husserlian tradition, not the Heideggerian, existential tradition. For Ingarden, "to intend" is to be *mentally* directed toward something, mentally directed in a perception, a thought, and so on. An intentional object, then, is the object of such an intention. By defining the LWA as an intentional object, Ingarden is aiming to overcome problems that arise in taking works of art to be ideal or physical objects. Ingarden's LWA is mind-dependent (ideal) but not a mere imaginary object; it transcends particular intentional acts. The LWA is what he calls a "stratified formation," consisting of both real and ideal components, which form an organic whole. Roughly speaking, the strata, the layers, are: (1) word sounds; (2) units of meaning; (3) schematized aspects; and (4) represented objects. I want to highlight the layer of schematized aspects. These are the many aspects of the subject matter that the author leaves incomplete, indeterminate, which the reader fleshes out, fills in through her reading experience. The reader's work of fleshing out this and other aspects of the LWA is what Ingarden calls "concretizing." The LWA—the *artistic* object—is to be distinguished from the *aesthetic* object; the latter is the intentional object that results from concretizing reading experiences. The LWA, then, is a potential aesthetic object. Ingarden's view provides interesting options for evaluation, since each layer of the LWA can be evaluated, as well as various interrelations among the layers, in terms of *artistic* value, while *aesthetic* value can be considered with respect to the aesthetic object.[54]

I do not want to venture too far into the specifics of Ingarden's theory. In fact, I want to draw upon only two features of it. First, I want to invoke the idea that the work of art may consist of more than one layer, each of which may be a different kind of thing. Second, drawing upon Ingarden's layer of schematized aspects, I want to consider the possibility that certain ingredients of a work of music may be present in the recorded sound *only in an incomplete manner*—incomplete in such a way that the listener's activity is required to complete it. We have seen that a groove requires a certain embodied, perceptual involvement. In order for the sounds musicians make to become grooves, they must be engaged with in a way that completes them. If something like this is right, then perhaps what we are entertaining is an extension of Gracyk's ontology of rock music. It would go something like this: the primary layer of the rock work is the recording; however, certain features, such as groove, must be made concrete in the experience of a listener, through her embodied engagement with the recording. (If we follow Ingarden further, we might say that certain lyrically represented objects, situations, and events are also incomplete in the recording.) This is a way to understand grooves to be essential features of musical works in certain contemporary genres, while emphasizing the perceiver's role in "concretizing" them. Grooves are schematized aspects of a recording. Grooves are present in a recording only schematically— they require a listener's embodied, active, aesthetic engagement to bring them to life.[55]

Back to the Beatles example

If my ontological suggestion is correct, the different grooves on the different versions of "Love Me Do" are essential features of two different works. From this ontological perspective, the grooves are not minor features of the recordings. George Martin was right to take the differences seriously. The "Love Me Do" debacle was caused by the lack of a way to understand grooves clearly enough to talk about them. It is interesting that, subsequently, the Beatles seemed to have no trouble intuiting their way around grooves. The "Love Me Do" situation was no doubt made worse by Ringo's nervousness (which made his playing worse), as well as his being asked to play a rhythmic pattern that is counter to his style. Later, in live performances, Ringo changes "Love Me Do" into a standard hi-hat shuffle, and plays it with a leaning-forward groove, always very smoothly.

What would have helped to avoid the debacle? Consider a suggestion by someone critical of my view. Perhaps some *analytical* attention to timing nuances might have helped. Ringo's version sounded disjointed and choppy partly because he was playing certain notes slightly late. It might have been suggested to him to strike those notes earlier. However, my point is that in order for any of this to be intelligible (to Ringo, Martin, or whomever) there would have to be some talk of the nonstructural effects of those nuances, namely, the fact that Ringo's groove has a backward-leaning *feel*, or that the target groove has a forward-leaning feel. But in order to talk about this, in order for such a feel to be intelligible, a listener has to "get" it, to feel it. And again, if someone does not understand the groove, encouraging the person to focus on certain notes that are a bit late is exactly the wrong way to help. If someone attempts to hear those certain notes *as* slightly late (analytically), then he will not experience the feel.[56] Let's say Martin was not so clear about what was wrong (or what was at the root of the disjointedness that he probably did notice). One of the other three Beatles might have said to Martin, "I know what's wrong with this, Ringo is making it lean backward instead of forward." As we have discussed, in order to help someone to comprehend/feel a groove, a person has to find the right perceptual structure. The fruit of my view is that we can communicate about this. By now, the reader knows the drill: we can suggest to Martin that he try tapping his foot to the pulse of Ringo's version, try *not* focusing on the second eighth note in the pair but perhaps the vocal, and so on. Ask Martin how he would describe the feel. Martin could have asked Ringo to do the same, and then he could have asked Ringo if he notices that the groove is a bit choppy. He could then ask Ringo to try a different groove, to make it lean forward or push more.

4.6 What a groove is: Conclusion

There are two aspects to the phenomenon of groove: the music (what a musician does to create a groove) and the felt dimension (a leaning feel, a pushing, a pulling, etc.). Let's consider the first aspect. To create a groove, a musician performs certain notes slightly early or slightly late; that is, a musician performs timing nuances (other elements may be involved, such as timbre, dynamics, shifting tempos, etc.). One difficulty in making sense of the phenomenon of groove is that one can perceive timing nuances in different ways, as is the case with many aspects of artworks in general (see 2.1). One, incorrect way to approach timing nuances is to approach them analytically (see 2.3), by scrutinizing the nuances in perception; this has the effect of separating them from their context. The consequence of this approach is that we perceive the notes as simply off-time, simply as late (say); we perceive notes that can accurately be described as "eighth note(-3)," "eighth note(+2)," and so on. I claim that musicians do not ordinarily engage with nuances analytically, and they certainly do not ordinarily intend for them to be heard in this way. Musicians who perform timing nuances are, no doubt, reflective about the fact that they are able to play notes slightly early or late, but if their objective is to generate or contribute to a groove, their focus is on the feel that is generated by the nuances—the feel of leaning, pushing, and so on—rather than the nuances themselves, perceived analytically. The feel is what confirms to a musician that she has accomplished what she set out to accomplish in performing a timing nuance, not an analytical perception of nuances. The feel is the perceptual datum that guides a musician's performance of nuances.

In the Introduction, I referred to four, pretheoretical intuitions about groove. The first is that grooves have a *feel*; a conspicuous affective dimension. These considerations confirm the second part of the first intuition: the feel of a groove is the dominant aspect of groove. Also, notice that perceiving nuances analytically is *derivative* upon perceiving them engagedly, in the sense that we wouldn't bother to look, nor know what we were looking for, if their effects had not first made an impression. This is to suggest, from another angle, that the feel of a groove is the dominant aspect.

In contrast to perceiving nuances analytically, we can perceive them in an ordinary manner, which I am calling "engagedly." Perceiving nuances engagedly results in hearing a performance's rhythm and early timing nuances *as* pushes, its late notes *as* pulls. Perceiving engagedly is not passive. Just as aesthetic experience in general is active (see 2.1), perceiving grooves is something we *do*. We must work to grasp the way the elements fit together qualitatively. When we perceive timing nuances analytically, the feel of the groove is absent, and we have no path toward it; we have no way to uncover a connection between the nuances and the feel. Perceiving engagedly involves exploring different ways of perceiving the various elements of a recording. The same element (say, a ride cymbal) can be perceived as in the background, or as the main feature in your experience (in addition, it can be perceived analytically, scrutinized). The *way* in which the cymbal sounds are perceived will have an effect on the experience as a whole. I argue in Chapter 2 that when certain nuance elements (cymbal sounds, bass guitar, kick drum, whatever) remain in the background of a perception (and if they remain indeterminate, ambiguous in perception), they can foster gestalts, such as a pushing groove—whereas, if you scrutinize that element, the gestalt will not emerge (see 2.6). These qualitative rhythmic gestalts (the pushing, pulling, and so on) are the musically significant phenomena, the nuances as analytically perceived are not.

So, one dimension of perceiving engagedly has to do with actively exploring and establishing an effective perceptual structure. The other, integrated dimension of perceiving engagedly has to do with the body.

The second, common intuition I mentioned in the Introduction is that grooves, in some sense, involve the body and its movement. To be sure, there are cases in which hearing music causes one's body to move. But I emphasize in Chapters 3 and 4 that conceiving of body movements as effects of hearing a rhythm is unhelpful in coming to understand the relationship between body movement and groove. We move our bodies *in order to* engage with rhythms. One way to approach conceiving of such a relationship is to notice that we have a way of comprehending certain objects, and managing certain tasks, through the movements of our bodies. For example, I have an understanding of the shape and flimsiness of this Coke can, by means of my fingers and thumb. My ability to deal with my computer's keyboard is not a matter of theoretical knowledge but a kind of knowledge *in my fingers*, knowledge that is *activated only in moving*. In these cases, my hands and fingers are intelligently *directed toward* these objects and tasks. This bodily sort of understanding is what Merleau-Ponty calls "motor intentionality"(3.4). Similarly, we come to understand a groove *through* an active, bodily engagement with a rhythm—foot-tapping to the pulse, head-bobbing, swaying, finger-snapping, and so on. I claim that understanding a groove requires body movement. But note that the motor-intentional activity involved in engaging with a groove is different from some other examples of motor intentionality. The groove cases are exploratory and repetitive, whereas the movement of (say) grasping a mug is less exploratory each time you take a drink. There is also an important difference in the role of the affective dimension of motor intentionality.

What is the nature of the feel of a groove? The feel of a groove is, in some sense, a bodily feeling. I make sense of this by emphasizing the affective dimension of motor intentionality. Motor-intentional activities are guided by bodily *feelings* (tensions, feelings of equilibrium, and so on) (see 3.5). One of Merleau-Ponty's examples is very instructive: when I view a painting in an art gallery I experience a bodily disequilibrium, a bodily tension, that guides me in moving forward or backward to an optimal viewing distance, at which point I feel a bodily equilibrium. Similarly, when I wrap my fingers around this Coke can, I feel in my hand, just as the can slips slightly, that I need to grip it more tightly. These bodily feelings inform our embodied, practical engagement with the world. *I claim that the feel of a groove just is the affective dimension of the relevant motor-intentional movements.* Comprehending a groove is unlike many other examples of motor intentionality due to the emphasis on this affective dimension. Unlike viewing a painting in an art gallery, typing, or grasping a mug, comprehending a groove places on a pedestal the affective dimension of motor intentionality. This is unsurprising, since experiences of grooves are aesthetic experiences, which means, at least, that we take the qualitative, affective dimension of the experience to be worthy of attention as an end in itself (see 4.1). But of course, the feel of a groove is not merely a quality of experience; it is a guide to noncognitively grasping the groove, as we discuss next.

The third common intuition about grooves is that to "get" a groove, to understand it, is not to apprehend it intellectually, in terms of some set of propositions or concepts; rather, to understand a groove is to feel it. Bodily understanding and feeling are intertwined in such a way in motor intentionality that the affective dimension of understanding a groove through movement *just is* the feel of a groove. One attempts to grasp a groove by moving to a pulse, which aids in setting a helpful perceptual structure. Moving to the pulse emphasizes the main beats in experience; the nuances recede into the perceptual background. The nuances are experienced not as (say) slightly late notes—as they would be perceived, if approached analytically—but rather, as pulls against the pulse, motor-intentional tensions, bodily feelings of disequilibrium, which are emphasized by the movement of the body. This is the general nature of the feel of grooves. Note the practical advice implied in this picture: if you find yourself unable to grasp a particular groove (perhaps a groove in a musical genre with which you are unfamiliar), experiment with moving your body to the pulse, explore variations of movement, observe the way others familiar with the genre move. Finding the right kinds of movements may begin to unlock, so to speak, the key perceptual structure, which will enable you to begin to experience what you previously perceived as off-time notes, now, as pushes, pulls—a groove (see 4.3).

Understanding a groove means to *feel* the qualitative relationships among the elements of the rhythm in one's body. This noncognitive grasping of a groove by moving to the pulse, and the feel that informs and guides this motor-intentional activity, are two sides of the same coin: to "get" a groove just is to comprehend it bodily and to feel that comprehension. The feel and the understanding come together in our bodily movement in a way that explains the fourth intuition: feeling a groove, and understanding it, does not occur through listening alone, nor in thinking, but *through the body*. To put this in yet another way, to feel a groove (the motor-intentional affect) occurs as we strive to understand the groove (motor-intentionally) through our body movement. Individuals in different musical cultures manifest different styles of movement, and there are differences between individuals within a given musical culture. I don't dispute this; I claim that the view I have set out provides an underlying and general way of understanding the relationships between movement, grasping grooves, and their feels (see 4.2).

I have also speculated about the role of grooves *in* music, in the terms of musical ontology (see 4.5). According to the traditional ontology of classical music, musical nuances and their effects (including the nonstructural, qualitative effects) are properties of performances only, not musical works. Musical works are structures, on this view, more or less represented in a score. An expanded ontology, which I favor, enables us to include, as features of the musical work, aspects of performance practices, conventions of notation, and so on. If we accept this ontology, then at least nuance types (but not specific nuances) are properties of some classical works. It stands to reason that the qualitative effects of some of these nuances are dominant, as we have shown regarding other genres (that is, what's important is not that a given note, analytically perceived, is late by such and such a degree; what's important is that it generates a pulling tension). Is body movement required in order to grasp these effects? This would seem to fly in the face of concert hall norms—but recall Stephen Davies's observations about the pervasiveness of body movement (see 3.2). Are there "grooves" in classical music? While they are less prominent in classical than in jazz and contemporary popular music, there are certainly qualities of pushing, pulling, leaning, and so on, in classical music. And in some cases, some of these feels may be properties of the works themselves.

Rock, hip-hop, and related genres require a different ontology. Theodore Gracyk's view is that rock musical works are the recordings themselves ("rock" is a broad category here). Recordings clearly include nuances. By considering the creative process in these genres, we see that the effects of nuances, including grooves, can even be more important than structural features; grooves are central features of rock works. By invoking two notions from Roman Ingarden's ontology of the literary work, I suggest an extension of Gracyk's ontology (see 4.5). Ingarden suggests that the literary work of art consists of different layers, and he suggests that one layer consists of incomplete ("schematized") aspects, which are fleshed-out, "concretized" by the reader. Taking "rock" very broadly, to include hip-hop and related styles, I suggest that the rock musical work involves at least two layers. The primary layer is the recording, but there is also a layer of incomplete features. Grooves are present in recordings only in an incomplete manner—incomplete in that a listener's activity is required to "concretize" them. Grooves are essential features of the musical works of many contemporary genres. In recordings and performances, grooves are present only schematically. Grooves are there in the music, but they may remain unnoticed by certain listeners. A groove is disclosed and concretized by a kind of motor-intentional skill, a facility for grasping the rhythm and its nuances, which culminates in an embodied aesthetic experience.

Notes

Introduction

1   On a biographical note, my experience with this exact perplexity, as a musician, had more than a little to do with my being driven to study philosophy.

2   Tiger Roholt, "*Musical* Musical Nuance," *The Journal of Aesthetics and Art Criticism* 68, no. 1 (Winter 2010): 1–10.

3   Tiger Roholt, "In Praise of Ambiguity: Merleau-Ponty and Musical Subtlety," *Contemporary Aesthetics* 11 (2013): http://www.contempaesthetics.org/newvolume/pages/article. php?articleID=669

4   Tiger Roholt, "Groove: The Phenomenology of Musical Nuance" (PhD diss., Columbia University, 2007).

5   "groove, n.", *OED Online*. December 2013. Oxford University Press. http://www.oed.com/view/Entry/81733?rskey=pt1h3H&result=1&isAd vanced=false (accessed January 24, 2014).

6   Led Zeppelin, "Blackdog," *Led Zeppelin IV* (Atlantic, 1994, compact disc. Originally released in 1971).

7   "Elephant," Tame Impala, *Lonerism* (Modular Recordings, 2012).

8   Frank Sinatra and Count Basie, "Fly Me to the Moon: In Other Words," *Sinatra at the Sands* (Warner Bros/WEA, 1998. Originally released in 1966).

9   Gene Vincent, "Race with the Devil," *The Screaming End: The Best Of Gene Vincent* (Razor & Tie, 1997, compact disc. Originally released in 1956).

10 The Beatles, "All My Lovin'," *With the Beatles* (Parlophone/Capitol, 1990, compact disc. Originally released in 1963).

11 P. Diddy, "Bad Boy for Life," *The Saga Continues* (Bad Boy, 2001, compact disc).

12 Brandy, "What About Us?" *Full Moon* (Urban Atlantic, 2004, compact disc).

13   Sinatra especially pulls against the rhythm when he sings, "Fly me
      to the moon; let me, swing among those stars. Let me see what
      spring is like on … Jupiter and Mars. In other words, hold my hand.
      In other words, baby *kiss* me." Sinatra and Basie, "Fly Me to the
      Moon."

14   "I remember when, I remember, I remember when I lost my mind.
      There was something so pleasant about that place, even your emotions
      have an echo in so much space." Gnarls Barkley, "Crazy," *St. Elsewhere*
      (Atlantic, 2006, compact disc).

15   Barry Kernfeld. "Groove (i)." *The New Grove Dictionary of Jazz, 2nd
      edn. Grove Music Online. Oxford Music Online.* Oxford University
      Press, http://www.oxfordmusiconline.com/subscriber/article/grove/
      music/J582400 (accessed January 25, 2014).

16   Charles Keil, "Participatory Discrepancies and the Power of Music,"
      in Charles Keil and Steven Feld, *Musical Grooves* (Tucson, Arizona:
      Fenstra, 2005), 98.

17   Richard Middleton, "Form," in *Key Terms in Popular Music and
      Culture*, eds Bruce Horner and Thom Swiss (Oxford: Blackwell, 1999),
      143.

18   Vijay Iyer, "Microstructures of Feel, Macrostructures of Sound:
      Embodied Cognition in West African and African-American Musics,"
      (PhD diss., University of California, Berkeley, 1998), chapter 2.

Chapter 1

1   The Beatles, *Anthology* (Capital, 2003, DVD. Originally released in
      1995).

2   For the session details, see Mark Lewisohn, *The Complete Beatles
      Recording Sessions: The Official Story of the Abbey Road Years
      1962–1970,* reprint edition (Sterling, 2013).

3   The Beatles, *Past Masters* (EMI, 2009, compact disc).

4   The Beatles, *Anthology.*

5   Geoff Emerick's recollection of the facts jibes with McCartney's. See
      Geoff Emerick and Howard Massey, *Here, There and Everywhere: My*

Life Recording the Music of the Beatles (New York: Penguin Books, 2006).

6   Tennessee Ernie Ford, "Sixteen Tons," *Vintage Collections Series* (EMI Special Products, 1997, compact disc).

7   Amy Winehouse, "Back to Black," *Back to Black* (Republic, 2007, compact disc).

8   Diana Raffman, *Language, Music, and Mind* (Cambridge, MA and London: MIT Press, 1993).

9   In a thoughtful review of Raffman's book, the music theorist Justin London criticizes her for not examining research on rhythm perception. He had the work of psychologists such as Eric Clarke in mind. See Justin London, "The Fine Art of Repetition: Essays in the Philosophy of Music; Language, Music, and Mind," *Music Theory Spectrum* 16, no. 2 (Autumn, 1994), 269.

10   Raffman, *Language, Music, and Mind*, 90.

11   Raffman, *Language, Music, and Mind*, 67, emphasis in original.

12   At the subsequent level of cognitive processing, Raffman understands the schematized pitches, chromatic pitches, to be the pitch input to Fred Lerdahl and Ray Jackendoff's Chomsky-like generative grammar of tonal music ("M-grammar"). Lerdahl and Jackendoff's M-grammar offers an explanation for an underlying competence that allows listeners to make sense of a string of tones; it is an account of just what a listener "does," subpersonally and unconsciously, to organize the musical surface into structured music. See Fred Lerdahl and Ray Jackendoff, *A Generative Theory of Tonal Music* (Cambridge, MA and London: MIT Press, 1983).

13   Vijay Iyer, "Microstructures of Feel, Macrostructures of Sound: Embodied Cognition in West African and African-American Musics" (PhD diss, University of California, Berkeley, 1998).

14   Vijay Iyer, "Embodied Mind, Situated Cognition, and Expressive Microtiming in African-American Music," *Music Perception* 19, no. 3 (2002): 387–414.

15   Christopher Peacocke, *Sense and Content* (Oxford: Clarendon Press, 1983), chapter 1.

16   Michael Tye, "Knowing What It Is Like: The Ability Hypothesis and

the Knowledge Argument," in *Reality and Humean Supervenience,* eds G. Preyer and F. Siebert (Lanham, MD: Rowman and Littlefield, 2000), Section 3.

17 See Gareth Evans, *The Varieties of Reference* (Oxford: Oxford University Press, 1982).

18 I am opting not to speak in terms of sound "onsets" for purposes of simplicity; this choice will not affect the examination.

19 Charles Keil, "Participatory Discrepancies and the Power of Music," in *Musical Grooves,* eds Charles Keil and Steven Feld (Tucson: Fenstra, 2005), 98. In his chapter in the same book, "Motion and Feeling through Music," Keil discusses *swing* as a more mysterious phenomenon (by "swing" he seems to be referring to groove); he considers the slight variations I am highlighting in the swing pattern. See pages 61–2.

20 Vijay Iyer, "Embodied Mind, Situated Cognition, and Expressive Microtiming in African-American Music," 398.

21 Vijay Iyer, "Embodied Mind, Situated Cognition, and Expressive Microtiming in African-American Music," 404.

22 "Crazy," Gnarls Barkley, *St. Elsewhere* (Atlantic, 2006, compact disc).

23 Frank Sinatra and Count Basie, "Fly Me to the Moon: In Other Words," *Sinatra at the Sands* (Warner Brothers/WEA, 1998, compact disc. Originally released in 1966).

24 Vijay Iyer, "Embodied Mind, Situated Cognition, and Expressive Microtiming in African-American Music," 388. In addition, consider this observation: "Gradually during the 1990s, in studying West African dance-drumming and in performing on keyboard instruments in jazz, hip-hop, and funk contexts, I experienced an interesting revelation: the simplest repetitive rhythmic patterns could be imbued with a universe of expression." Iyer, "Embodied Mind, Situated Cognition, and Expressive Microtiming in African-American Music," 396.

25 Iyer, "Embodied Mind, Situated Cognition, and Expressive Microtiming in African-American Music," 410.

26 Raffman, *Language, Music, and Mind,* 2.

27 Raffman, *Language, Music, and Mind,* 3.

28 Raffman, *Language, Music, and Mind,* 3, emphasis added.

29 Raffman, *Language, Music, and Mind,* 84, emphasis in original. One
    might wonder whether experienced musicians can improve their
    abilities to recognize nuance pitches (etc.). Some of Raffman's critics
    (e.g. Justin London) seem not to have noticed that she addresses
    this. See Justin London, "The Fine Art of Repetition: Essays in the
    Philosophy of Music; Language, Music, and Mind," 269–75. Raffman
    cites findings to the effect that even Indian musicians, whose scales
    are microtonal, are unable to reliably categorize more finely than
    semitones. The main point is that although we may acquire more
    finely-tuned schemas, "it is overwhelmingly unlikely that we could
    acquire interval schemas as fine-grained as the pitch and interval
    discriminations we can make." Raffman, *Language, Music, and Mind,*
    84. Also consider: "The limits of our schemas are the limits of our
    language, and qua perceivers we are so designed that the grain of
    conscious experience will inevitably be finer than that of our schemas,
    no matter how long, or how diligently, we practice." Raffman,
    Language, Music, and Mind, 136.
30 Raffman, *Language, Music, and Mind,* 83.
31 W. E. Kennick, "Art and the Ineffable," *Journal of Philosophy* 58 (1961):
    309–20.
32 Kennick, "Art and the Ineffable," 317–18.
33 Ludwig Wittgenstein, *The Blue and Brown Books,* 2nd edn (Oxford:
    Blackwell, 1998).
34 Wittgenstein, *The Blue and Brown Books,* 181.
35 Wittgenstein, *The Blue and Brown Books,* 181.
36 Raffman, *Language, Music, and Mind,* 140, emphasis in original.
37 Georges Rey, "Review of *Language, Music, and Mind,*" *The
    Philosophical Review* 106 (1997): 641–5.
38 Rey, "Review of *Language, Music, and Mind,*" 643.
39 Raffman, *Language, Music, and Mind,* 66, emphasis in original.
40 Raffman, *Language, Music, and Mind,* 86.
41 Eric F. Clarke, "The Perception of Expressive Timing in Music,"
    Psychological Research 51 (1989): 2–9, quotation from page 3. Vijay
    Iyer maintains that there are three "roles" played by microtiming in the
    groove-based music he considers; similar to Raffman and Clarke, the

first role he mentions is to emphasize structural features of the music. Regarding a swing rhythm in general, as we have seen, the second eighth note is shorter than the first (as compared with a rhythm consisting of straight eighth notes that are not swung). Iyer claims that the role of the swing rhythm in general is the resulting emphasis of the pulse. This emphasis is taken a step further with the addition of microtimings. Iyer writes, "But the point is that this difference facilitates the perception of higher level rhythmic structure. An immediate consequence of the swing feel is that it suggests the next level of hierarchical organization. In conventional terms, the swung eighth-note pairs are perceptually grouped into the larger regular interval, that is, the quarter note. If all subdivisions were performed with exactly the same duration, it would be more difficult to perceive the main beat. The lengthening of the first of two swung notes in a pair amounts to a durational accentuation of the beat. ... Hence swing enhances the perception of the main pulse." Iyer, "Embodied Mind, Situated Cognition, and Expressive Microtiming in African-American Music," 404.

42   Raffman writes, "The structural description is so called because it represents the signal as instantiating the basic structural elements of the music—namely its pitches and rhythms—as well as the more abstract structural features inferred therefrom. In calling these the structural features, I mean inter alia that they constitute a system of elements whose tokens are: (1) discrete; (2) type-identifiable by some finite mechanical procedure; and (3) combinable in certain role-governed ways. ... The structural description does not, at least not explicitly, capture what I shall call the nonstructural features of the music. Dynamics (loudness levels), tempi (perceived speeds), and timbres (tone 'colors') come immediately to mind. ... For the time being I shall characterize the nonstructural features, unhelpfully, as those audible features of the music that fail to satisfy the trio of conditions just cited." Raffman, *Language, Music, and Mind*, 25. The more thorough characterization of nonstructural features Raffman signals here turns out to be her account of nuances. Unfortunately, as we have seen, she understands these to be discrete properties that are characterizable in terms of direct description.

43   Some minute variations in pitch and timing have timbral effects (objectives), and some timbral adjustments contribute to more global timbral effects. These sound qualities are central in rock (broadly construed), as Gracyk emphasizes: "Rock is a music of very specific sound qualities and their textural combination. Specific sounds are as central to the music as are specific colors in painting." Theodore Gracyk, *Rhythm and Noise: An Aesthetics of Rock* (London and New York: I. B. Tauris, 1996), 61. For more on Gracyk's ontology of rock music, see 4.5.

44   This picture emerges from my own experience; this is, at least, a way that some rock musicians deal with musical nuances. I certainly do not mean to imply that classical musicians are less conscious of nuances.

45   Something similar may occur in classical composition but the nuance considerations, I believe, are less specific; the considerations would be limited to *types* of nuances (cashed out in terms of performance practices and, perhaps, stipulated in a score's supplementary instructions). For more, see 4.5.

46   For a discussion of my claims about ineffability in my "*Musical Musical Nuance*," see John Spackman, "Expressiveness, Ineffability, and Nonconceptuality," *The Journal of Aesthetics and Art Criticism* 70, no. 3 (Summer 2012).

47   Although Vijay Iyer's analyses of timing nuances are conducted in terms similar to Raffman's, he acknowledges the importance of the *effects* of nuances more explicitly than Raffman: "All these musical quantities combine dynamically and holistically to form what some would call a musician's 'feel.' Individual players have their own feel, that is, their own ways of relating to an isochronous pulse." Vijay Iyer, "Embodied Mind, Situated Cognition, and Expressive Microtiming in African-American Music," 398.

48   Marty Robbins, "El Paso," *Gunfighter Ballads and Trail Songs* (Sony, 1999, compact disc).

Chapter 2

1   Clive Bell, *Art* (Oxford University Press, 1987), 9. Originally published in 1914.

2   Roman Ingarden, "Phenomenological Aesthetics: An Attempt at Defining Its Range," *The Journal of Aesthetics and Art Criticism* 33, no. 3 (1975): 261.

3   R. G. Collingwood, *The Principles of Art* (New York: Oxford University Press, 1958), 140–1. Originally published in 1938.

4   John Dewey, *Art as Experience* (New York: Perigee, 1980), 53. Originally published in 1934.

5   John Dewey, *Art as Experience*, 54. Dewey is also emphasizing here that aesthetic experiences are ends in themselves.

6   Steven Feld, "Aesthetics as Iconicity of Style (Uptown Title); Or, (Downtown Title) 'Lift-Up-Over Sounding': Getting into the Kaluli Groove," in Charles Keil and Steven Feld, eds, *Musical Grooves* (Tucson, AZ: Fenstra, 2005), 111.

7   See Justin London, *Hearing in Time: Psychological Aspects of Musical Meter*, 2nd edn (Oxford: Oxford University Press, 2012).

8   Daniel Dennett, "Quining Qualia," in *Philosophy of Mind: Classical and Contemporary Readings*, ed. David J. Chalmers (Oxford: Oxford University Press, 2002).

9   Dennett, "Quining Qualia," 243–4.

10 Dennett, "Quining Qualia," 244.

11 Maurice Merleau-Ponty, *Phenomenology of Perception*, trans. Donald A. Landes (London and New York: Routledge, 2012), 4. Originally published in 1945.

12 Merleau-Ponty, *Phenomenology of Perception*, 275.

13 Merleau-Ponty, *Phenomenology of Perception*, 32.

14 Eric F. Clarke, "The Perception of Expressive Timing in Music," *Psychological Research* 51: 2–9 (1989), 3.

15 Raffman, *Language, Music, and Mind*, 65. Raffman is here drawing from E. M. Burns and W. D. Ward, "Intervals, Scales, and Tuning," in *The Psychology of Music*, ed. Diana Deutsch (San Diego: Elsevier, 1982), 241–69.

16   Raffman, *Language, Music, and Mind*, 140.

17   Consider these further comments by Raffman: "Do not
     misunderstand: certainly we could coin (type-identifying) names
     for the N-pitches—names like, say, 'A-natural(1)', 'A-natural(12)',
     'B-flat(10)', and so forth—just as we could coin names for all the
     determinate shades we can see. But for want of the requisite schemas
     in long-term memory, we would not be able to apply those names 'by
     ear'. In this respect the nuances are known ineffably—are, as I shall say,
     nuance ineffable." Raffman, *Language, Music, and Mind*, 88. For more
     on Raffman's ineffability claim, see Roholt, "*Musical*, Musical Nuance,"
     The Journal of Aesthetics and Art Criticism 68 (2010): 1–10.

18   Prior to Merleau-Ponty, the gestalt psychologist Kurt Koffka uses the
     term "analytical attitude," drawing a similar distinction.

19   Merleau-Ponty, *Phenomenology of Perception*, 247.

20   Merleau-Ponty, *Phenomenology of Perception*, 235.

21   Merleau-Ponty, *Phenomenology of Perception*, 48.

22   Merleau-Ponty, *Phenomenology of Perception*, 235.

23   Merleau-Ponty, *Phenomenology of Perception*, 235, emphasis in
     original.

24   See Merleau-Ponty, *Phenomenology of Perception*, 234–5.

25   Merleau-Ponty, *Phenomenology of Perception*, 235.

26   Merleau-Ponty, *Phenomenology of Perception*, 235, emphasis in
     original.

27   Merleau-Ponty, *Phenomenology of Perception*, 307.

28   "The determinate quality by which empiricism wanted to define
     sensation is an object for, not an element of consciousness, and it is
     the recently introduced object of scientific consciousness." Merleau-
     Ponty, *Phenomenology of Perception*, 7.

29   Merleau-Ponty, *Phenomenology of Perception*, 500 n. 24.

30   Merleau-Ponty, "The Film and the New Psychology," in *Sense
     and Non-Sense*, eds H. L. Dreyfus and P. A. Dreyfus (Evanston:
     Northwestern University Press, 1964), 49.

31   Merleau-Ponty, "The Film and the New Psychology," 49.

32   Lester Embree, "Merleau-Ponty's Examination of Gestalt Psychology,"
     Research in Phenomenology 10 (1980), 13.

33 Embree, "Merleau-Ponty's Examination of Gestalt Psychology," 5.

34 Merleau-Ponty, *The Structure of Behavior*, trans. Alden L. Fisher (Boston: Beacon Press, 1963), 168. Quoted in Embree, "Merleau-Ponty's Examination of Gestalt Psychology," 5.

35 Embree, "Merleau-Ponty's Examination of Gestalt Psychology," 6.

36 "Our original (primitive) perception bears more on relations than on isolated terms." Embree, "Merleau-Ponty's Examination of Gestalt Psychology," 14.

37 In her book, Raffman criticizes Dennett on other grounds: for not acknowledging that we can discriminate more finely than we can conceptualize. See her Chapter 7, "Qualms about Quining Qualia."

38 Raffman, *Language, Music, and Mind*, 66.

39 See Sean D. Kelly, "Edmund Husserl and Phenomenology," in *The Blackwell Guide to Continental Philosophy*, eds Robert C. Solomon and David Sherman (Oxford: Blackwell, 2003).

40 Sean D. Kelly, "Seeing Things in Merleau-Ponty," in *The Cambridge Companion to Merleau-Ponty*, eds Taylor C. Carman and Mark B. N. Hansen (Cambridge: Cambridge University Press, 2005), 81.

41 Merleau-Ponty, *Phenomenology of Perception*, 6. Kelly draws upon a portion of this quotation; I am adopting Kelly's adjustment to the translation (see pages 80–1 of his "Seeing Things in Merleau-Ponty"). The visual field includes objects of attention as well as the background; Merleau-Ponty's conception of the perceptual background is obviously quite broad.

42 Merleau-Ponty, "The Film and the New Psychology," 51, emphasis in original.

43 Kelly, "Seeing Things in Merleau-Ponty," 82, emphasis in original.

44 Kelly, "Seeing Things in Merleau-Ponty," 82ff, emphasis in original.

45 See Merleau-Ponty, *Phenomenology of Perception*, 7.

46 See Merleau-Ponty, *Phenomenology of Perception*, 8.

47 Merleau-Ponty, *Phenomenology of Perception*, 11, emphasis added.

48 Plato, *The Republic*, trans. C. D. C. Reeve and G. M. A. Grube (Indianapolis and Cambridge: Hackett, 1992), 523a.

49 Merleau-Ponty, *Phenomenology of Perception*, 7.

50 Lorde, "Royals," *Pure Heroine* (Universal Music Group, 2013).

51 Clarke, "The Perception of Expressive Timing in Music," 3.
52 Merleau-Ponty, *Phenomenology of Perception*, 322.
53 Merleau-Ponty, *Phenomenology of Perception*, 322–3.
54 Merleau-Ponty, *Phenomenology of Perception*, 323, emphasis in original.
55 Merleau-Ponty, *Phenomenology of Perception*, 7.
56 Charles Keil, "Participatory Discrepancies and the Power of Music." In *Musical Grooves,* eds Charles Keil and Steven Feld (Tucson, AZ: Fenstra, 2005), 103–4, emphasis in original.
57 Keil and Feld, *Musical Grooves*, 155.
58 J. A. Prögler, "Searching for Swing: Participatory Discrepancies in the Jazz Rhythm Section," *Ethnomusicology* 39, no. 1, Special Issue: *Participatory Discrepancies* (Winter, 1995), 21–54.
59 Prögler, "Searching for Swing: Participatory Discrepancies in the Jazz Rhythm Section," 21.
60 Prögler, "Searching for Swing: Participatory Discrepancies in the Jazz Rhythm Section," 35.
61 Charles Keil, "Theory of Participatory Discrepancies: a Progress Report" *Ethnomusicology* 39, no. 1, Special Issue: *Participatory Discrepancies* (Winter, 1995), 2–3.
62 Iyer, "Embodied Mind, Situated Cognition, and Expressive Microtiming in African-American Music," 388.
63 Iyer, "Embodied Mind, Situated Cognition, and Expressive Microtiming in African-American Music," 410.
64 Although he is not considering perception as distinguished from playing in these pages, on 395–6 of his "Embodied Mind, Situated Cognition, and Expressive Microtiming in African-American Music," Iyer comes closest to noticing the importance of conceiving of our relationship to grooves as being something less than determinate. But again, the focus on these pages is upon *performing* rhythms with micro-timings.
65 Paul Cézanne, *Madame Cézanne in a Yellow Chair,* 1888–90. Chicago Institute of Art.
66 Paul Cézanne, *Madame Cézanne in a Red Dress,* 1888–90. Metropolitan Museum of Art.

67   Roger Fry, *Cézanne: A Study of His Development* (New York: Macmillan, 1927), 68.

68   Paul Cézanne, *Madame Cézanne with Green Hat,* 1891–92. The Barnes Foundation.

69   Half in jest, the philosopher of mind, Ned Block, when considering what philosophers mean by qualia, quoted Armstrong. The quote comes from Ned Block, "Troubles with Functionalism," in *Readings in Philosophy of Psychology*, volume 1. ed. Ned Block, (Cambridge: Harvard University Press, 1980) 278.

70   Friedrich Wilhelm Nietzsche, *The Gay Science*, ed. Bernard Williams; trans. Josefine Nauckhoff (Cambridge and New York: Cambridge University Press, 2001), section 373.

Chapter 3

1   Thomas Mathiesen, "Ancient Greek Music," in *The Oxford Companion to Music*. Oxford Music Online. Oxford University Press, http://www.oxfordmusiconline.com/subscriber/article/opr/t114/e260 (accessed February 1, 2014).

2   Baugh, Bruce, "Prolegomena to Any Aesthetics of Rock Music," *The Journal of Aesthetics and Art Criticism* 51 (1993): 23–9.

3   In my view, Baugh's paper is an interesting and important attempt at exploring the right territory, and a valiant effort to avoid the traditional, analytical mistakes. But unfortunately, due to the limited and restrictive philosophical tools he employs, his essay is somewhat unclear, and would be unfruitful to consider in more depth for our purposes.

4   Stephen Davies, "Rock Versus Classical Music," *Journal of Aesthetics and Art Criticism* 57, no. 2 (1999): 193–204.

5   Davies, "Rock Versus Classical Music," 197.

6   Davies, "Rock Versus Classical Music," 197, emphasis added.

7   Justin London, "Pulse," in *Grove Music Online*, ed. L. Macy, http://www.oxfordmusiconline.com/subscriber/article/grove/music/45964 (accessed June 1, 2013). Also see Gracyk, *Rhythm and Noise; an Aesthetics of Rock*, 131.

8   Fred Lerdahl and Ray Jackendoff, *A Generative Theory of Tonal Music* (Cambridge, MA and London: MIT Press, 1983), 71.

9   Lee B. Brown, "The Theory of Jazz Music; 'It Don't Mean a Thing …'" *The Journal of Aesthetics and Art Criticism* 49, no. 2 (1991): 120.

10 Iyer, "Embodied Mind, Situated Cognition, and Expressive Microtiming in African-American Music," 388.

11 Iyer, "Embodied Mind, Situated Cognition, and Expressive Microtiming in African-American Music," 389, emphasis in original.

12 Iyer also draws upon the perspective of situated cognition; set this aside for my Chapter 4.

13 See Chapter 4 of Iyer, *Microstructures of Feel, Macrostructures of Sound: Embodied Cognition in West African and African-American Musics.*

14 Iyer, "Embodied Mind, Situated Cognition, and Expressive Microtiming in African-American Music", 392, quoting from N. P. M. Todd, "Motion in music: A neurobiological perspective," *Music Perception* 17 (1999): 115–26. The emphasis is from the original, and it is exactly the phrase I would like to emphasize. Manifesting similar shortcomings for our purposes is B. Carroll-Phelan and P. J. Hampson, "Multiple Components of the Perception of Musical Sequences: A Cognitive Neuroscience Analysis and Some implications for Auditory Imagery," *Music Perception* 13 (1996): 517–61.

15 Iyer, "Embodied Mind, Situated Cognition, and Expressive Microtiming in African-American Music," 392, emphasis added.

16 Iyer, "Embodied Mind, Situated Cognition, and Expressive Microtiming in African-American Music, 392," emphasis added.

17 For instance, Iyer cites N. P. M. Todd, "The Auditory 'Primal Sketch': A Multiscale Model of Rhythmic Grouping," *Journal of New Music Research* 23 (1994): 25–70.

18 Iyer, "Embodied Mind, Situated Cognition, and Expressive Microtiming in African-American Music," 393.

19 Iyer, "Embodied Mind, Situated Cognition, and Expressive Microtiming in African-American Music," 407.

20 Iyer, *Microstructures of Feel, Macrostructures of Sound: Embodied Cognition in West African and African-American Musics,* chapter 4.

Doc Cheatham quotation from P. Berliner, *Thinking in Jazz: The Infinite Art of Improvisation* (Chicago: University of Chicago Press, 1994), 152.

21 See Howard Robinson, *Perception* (London and New York: Routledge, 1994), chapter 1.

22 Lawrence Hass, *Merleau-Ponty's Philosophy* (Bloomington and Indianapolis: Indiana University Press, 2008), 22.

23 Taylor Carman, *Merleau-Ponty* (London and New York: Routledge, 2008), 84.

24 Merleau-Ponty, *Phenomenology of Perception*, 141.

25 Carman, *Merleau-Ponty*, 19.

26 Carman, *Merleau-Ponty*, 87. Again, "The body … cannot be understood as a mere causal link in a chain of events that terminates in perceptual experience." Carman, *Merleau-Ponty*, 1.

27 Joseph Rouse, "Coping and Its Contrasts," in *Heidegger, Coping, and Cognitive Science: Essays in Honor of Hubert L. Dreyfus*, volume 2, eds Mark A. Wrathall and Jeff Malpas (Cambridge, MA and London: MIT Press, 2000), 12.

28 See Kelly, "Grasping at Straws: Motor Intentionality and the Cognitive Science of Skilled Behavior," in *Heidegger, Coping, and Cognitive Science: Essays in Honor of Hubert L. Dreyfus*, volume 2, 176.

29 For more on motor intentionality, see Sean D. Kelly, "Merleau-Ponty on the Body: The Logic of Motor Intentional Activity," *Ratio* XV, no. 4 (2002): 376–91.

30 More properly, such movements are directed toward a *world*, in the Heideggerian sense. Merleau-Ponty writes, "Vision and movement are specific ways of relating to objects and, if a single function is expressed throughout all of these experiences, then it is the movement of existence, which does not suppress the radical diversity of contents, for it does not unite them by placing them all under the domination of an 'I think', but rather by orienting them toward the intersensory unity of a world. Movement is not a movement in thought, and bodily space is not a space that is conceived or represented." Merleau-Ponty, *Phenomenology of Perception*, 139.

31 Merleau-Ponty, *Phenomenology of Perception*, 140.

32 Rouse, "Coping and Its Contrasts," 9.

33   Sean Kelly emphasizes that we cannot explain such intentional behavior in terms of reflexes, as the empiricist attempts: see Sean D. Kelly, "Grasping at Straws: Motor Intentionality and the Cognitive Science of Skilled Behavior," 166–7.

34   See Hubert Dreyfus's "Responses," chapter 16 in *Heidegger, Coping, and Cognitive Science: Essays in Honor of Hubert L. Dreyfus*, volume 2, 328.

35   Merleau-Ponty, *Phenomenology of Perception*, 139.

36   "What Merleau-Ponty calls the 'phenomenal field' is neither a representation nor a locus of representations, but a dimension of our bodily embeddedness in a perceptually coherent environment, a primitive aspect of our openness onto the world." Carman, "Sensation, Judgment, and the Phenomenal Field," 51.

37   Although Martin Heidegger does not consider the body at any length in *Being and Time*, he places similar emphasis on a kind of practical, engaged understanding of our environment, which he terms "readiness-to-hand" (*Zuhandenheit*)—as opposed to the more analytical, "presence-at-hand" (*Vorhandenheit*). See Martin Heidegger, *Being and Time*, trans. John Macquarrie and Edward Robinson (New York: Harper Perennial Modern Classics, 2008). Originally published in 1927. Also see Carman, *Merleau-Ponty*, 224.

38   Carman, *Merleau-Ponty,* 36, 37, emphasis in original. Further, "The body is not just a causal but a transcendental condition of perception, which is itself not just an inner subjective state, but a mode of being in the world." Carman, *Merleau-Ponty*, 82.

39   E. Matthews, *The Philosophy of Merleau-Ponty* (Montreal and Kingston: McGill-Queen's University Press, 2002), 49.

40   Carman, *Merleau-Ponty*, 110, emphasis added.

41   Merleau-Ponty, *Phenomenology of Perception*, 315–16, emphasis added. A portion of this passage is quoted in Sean D. Kelly, "Husserl and Phenomenology," in *The Blackwell Guide to Continental Philosophy*, ed. Robert C. Solomon (Oxford: Blackwell Publishers, 2003), 128.

42   Carman, *Merleau-Ponty*, 110–11, emphasis in original. Also: "The *body schema* [is] the set of abiding noncognitive dispositions and capacities that orient, guide, and inform our bodily sensitivities and motor

actions. To say that perception is grounded in the body is to say that the phenomenal field is constituted by the body schema. Our bodily skills and dispositions carve out a perceptual world with perspectival horizons and a contrast between figure and ground." Carman, *Merleau-Ponty*, 132–3.

43 Carman, *Merleau-Ponty*, 110. A particularly helpful discussion of these epistemic issues can be found in Charles Taylor, "Merleau-Ponty and The Epistemological Picture," in *The Cambridge Companion to Merleau-Ponty*, eds Taylor Carman and Mark Hansen (Cambridge: Cambridge University Press, 2005).

44 Merleau-Ponty, *Phenomenology of Perception*, 145, emphasis in original.

45 Kelly, "Edmund Husserl and Phenomenology," in *The Blackwell Guide to Continental Philosophy*, eds Robert C. Solomon and David Sherman (Oxford: Blackwell, 2003), 132.

46 Kelly, "Edmund Husserl and Phenomenology," 132.

47 Kelly, "Edmund Husserl and Phenomenology," 129.

Chapter 4

1 I remain grateful to Sean Kelly for pressing me to find solutions to core problems in this project through Merleau-Ponty.

2 Merleau-Ponty, *Phenomenology of Perception*, 315–16.

3 Hubert Dreyfus, "Merleau-Ponty and Recent Cognitive Science," in *The Cambridge Companion to Merleau-Ponty*, eds Taylor Carman and Mark Hansen (Cambridge: Cambridge University Press, 2005), 137.

4 Merleau-Ponty rejects the general notion that we can understand the relationship between that which we perceive and the body (and its movement) in cause effect terms: "Let us be more precise. The sensing being and the sensible are not opposite each other like two external terms, and sensation does not consist of the sensible invading the sensing being. My gaze subtends color, the movement of my hand subtends the form of the object, or rather my gaze pairs off with the color and my hand with the hard and the soft. In this exchange

between the subject of sensation and the sensible, it cannot be said that one acts while the other suffers the action, nor that one gives sense to the other. Without the exploration of my gaze or my hand, and prior to my body synchronizing with it, the sensible is nothing but a vague solicitation." After introducing the example of perceiving determinate colors, Merleau-Ponty writes, "Thus, a sensible that is about to be sensed poses to my body a sort of confused problem. I must find the attitude that *will* provide it with the means to become determinate and to become blue; I must find the response to a poorly formulated question." Merleau-Ponty, *Phenomenology of Perception*, 221–2.

5 To be clear, I am not claiming that the rhythmic elements we find in a recording or performance are machine-perfect, with only one nuanced, rhythmic element. What I have been focusing upon is the tension of a pulse against nuances.

6 See John Dewey, *Art as Experience* (New York: Perigee, 1980). Originally published in 1934). Also see Monroe Beardsley, *The Aesthetic Point of View*, eds M. Wreen and D. Callen (Ithaca, NY: Cornell University Press, 1982).

7 Dewey holds that an aesthetic experience is unified. It possesses a pervasive quality. An aesthetic experience is a complete experience, continuing until it reaches a consummation. See John Dewey, *Art as Experience*. For overviews of the concept of aesthetic experience, and the aesthetic experience theories of John Dewey and Monroe Beardsley, see the relevant entries in my *Key Terms in Philosophy of Art* (London: Bloomsbury Academic, 2013).

8 This is a Heideggerian point. Shaun Gallagher and Dan Zahavi write, "When I play ping-pong, my movements are not given as intentional objects. My limbs do not compete with the ball for my attention. If that were the case, I would be unable to play efficiently ... [O]ur attention, our intentional focus, is normally on the task to be performed, the project to be accomplished, or on some worldly event that seems relevant to our action. Our attention is not on our bodily movement." Shaun Gallagher and Dan Zahavi, *The Phenomenological Mind: An Introduction to Philosophy of Mind and Cognitive Science* (London and New York: Routledge, 2008), 145.

9   Rouse, "Coping and Its Contrasts," 12
10 Davies, "Rock Versus Classical Music," 197.
11 Quoted in Keil and Feld, *Musical Grooves* (Tucson, AZ: Fenstra, 2005), 111 n. 2.
12 The Beatles, "All My Lovin'," *With the Beatles* (Parlophone/Capitol, 1990).
13 Sly and The Family Stone, "Thank You (Falettinme Be Mice Elf Agin)," *Greatest Hits* (Epic Records, 1970).
14 Richard Shusterman, "Don't Believe the Hype," in Richard Shusterman, *Performing Live: Aesthetic Alternatives for the Ends of Art* (Ithaca and London: Cornell University Press, 2000), 44.
15 Richard Shusterman, "Don't Believe the Hype," 44, emphasis added.
16 Richard Shusterman, *Thinking Through the Body: Essays in Somaesthetics* (Cambridge and New York: Cambridge University Press, 2012), 3. Shusterman is quoting Merleau-Ponty: Merleau-Ponty, *Phenomenology of Perception*, xiv. And Maurice Merleau-Ponty, *In Praise of Philosophy and Other Essays*, trans. John Wild, James Edie, and John O'Neill (Evanston, IL: Northwestern University Press, 1970), 63. In addition, in this light, Shusterman writes, "Even our most basic nondiscursive experiences are significantly shaped by the cultures and environments we inhabit, and these are neither uniform nor unchanging. We are already shaped by culture in the womb." Shusterman, *Thinking Through the Body*, 195.
17 Iyer, "Embodied Mind, Situated Cognition, and Expressive Microtiming in African-American Music," 388.
18 See Pierre Bourdieu, *Distinction: A Social Critique of the Judgement of Taste*, trans. R. Nice (Cambridge, MA: Harvard University Press, 1984 [1979]). Also see Pierre Bourdieu, "The Historical Genesis of a Pure Aesthetic," *The Journal of Aesthetics and Art Criticism* 46 (1987): 201–10. One can find interesting discussions of Bourdieu in Richard Shusterman, *Performing Live: Aesthetic Alternatives for the Ends of Art* (Ithaca, NY and London: Cornell University Press, 2000). In addition, see Theodore Gracyk, *Listening to Popular Music: Or, How I Learned to Stop Worrying and Love Led Zeppelin* (Ann Arbor: The University of Michigan Press, 2007).
19 See Carman, *Merleau-Ponty*, chapter 7.

20 See my "Continental Philosophy and Music," in Theodore Gracyk and Andrew Kania, eds, *The Routledge Companion to Philosophy and Music* (London and New York: Routledge, 2011).

21 See Shusterman, "Don't Believe the Hype," especially pages 53–9, in Richard Shusterman, *Performing Live: Aesthetic Alternatives for the Ends of Art* (Ithaca, NY and London: Cornell University Press, 2000).

22 Martin Clayton, Rebecca Sager and Udo Will, "In Time With The Music: The Concept of Entrainment and its Significance for Ethnomusicology," *ESEM Counterpoint II* (2005): 2.

23 What is meter? Here is the beginning of the *Grove Music Online* entry, "Metre": "(1) A synonym for time signature as in '6/8 metre'. (2) More generally, the temporal hierarchy of subdivisions, beats and bars that is maintained by performers and inferred by listeners which functions as a dynamic temporal framework for the production and comprehension of musical durations. In this sense, metre is more an aspect of the behaviour of performers and listeners than an aspect of the music itself." Justin London, "Metre," *Grove Music Online. Oxford Music Online.* Oxford University Press, http://www.oxfordmusiconline.com/subscriber/article/grove/music/18519 (accessed February 15, 2014).

24 London, *Hearing in Time: Psychological Aspects of Musical Meter*, 2nd edn, (Oxford: Oxford University Press, 2012).

25 Quoted in London, *Hearing in Time*, 11. Mari Riess Jones, "Attentional Rhythmicity in Human Perception," in *Rhythm in Psychological, Linguistic, and Musical Processes*, eds J. R. Evans and M. Clynes (Springfield, IL: Thomas, 1986).

26 Jones, quoted in London, *Hearing in Time*, 12; quoted from Mari Riess Jones, "Time, Our Lost Dimension: Toward a New Theory of Perception, Attention, and Memory," *Psychological Review* 83, no. 5 (1976): 323–55.

27 Large, quoted in London, *Hearing in Time*, 48; quoted from Edward W. Large, "Resonating to Musical Rhythm: Theory and Experiment," in *Psychology of Time*, ed. Simon Grondin (Bingly, UK: Emerald Group Publishing Ltd, 2008).

28 London, *Hearing in Time*, 48.

29 Iyer, "Embodied Mind, Situated Cognition, and Expressive Microtiming in African-American Music," 392, quoting from N. P. M. Todd, "Motion

in Music: A Neurobiological Perspective" *Music Perception* 17 (1999): 115–26, emphasis in original.

30 London, *Hearing in Time,* 32, emphasis added.

31 London, *Hearing in Time,* 22, emphasis added.

32 Justin London takes the quintessential example of temporal entrainment to be foot-tapping. See Justin London, *Hearing in Time,* 48 and 12.

33 For this quotation, Iyer cites his personal communication with M. Bilal, 1997. Emphasis added.

34 Iyer, "Embodied Mind, Situated Cognition, and Expressive Microtiming in African-American Music," 391–2, emphasis added.

35 Dr. Dre, "Forgot about Dre," 2001 (*Aftermath*, Interscope, 1999).

36 Brandy, *Full Moon* (Urban Atlantic, 2004).

37 There are problems with this view; for example, there are questions about the extent to which perceivers constitute certain features of a work of art. A work of art has properties that the painted canvas does not. I'll set these issues aside here, but they emerge regarding musical works below.

38 See, for example, the description in Stephen Davies, *Musical Works and Performances* (Oxford: Oxford University Press, 2001), 100 and 10.

39 Raffman, *Language, Music, and Mind,* 65.

40 See Davies, *Musical Works and Performances,* 106–7.

41 Davies, *Musical Works and Performances,* 4–5.

42 Davies, *Musical Works and Performances,* 107.

43 Davies, *Musical Works and Performances,* 105–6.

44 Lydia Goehr, *The Imaginary Museum of Musical Works* (Oxford: Clarendon Press, 1994). For a summary of some central aspects of Goehr's position, see my "Continental Philosophy and Music," in *The Routledge Companion to Philosophy and Music,* eds Theodore Gracyk and Andrew Kania (London and New York: Routledge, 2011).

45 For a relevant discussion, see Stephen Davies, *Musical Works and Performances* (Oxford: Oxford University Press, 2001), 110 and 116.

46 Theodore Gracyk, *Rhythm and Noise: an Aesthetics of Rock* (London: I. B. Tauris, 1996), 58, quoting John Shepherd.

47 Gracyk, *Rhythm and Noise,* 61.

48 Gracyk, *Rhythm and Noise,* 57.

49 Gracyk, *Rhythm and Noise*, 1; also see Davies, *Musical Works and Performances*, 30.

50 Gracyk, *Rhythm and Noise*, 12.

51 Stephen Davies, "Rock Versus Classical Music," *Journal of Aesthetics and Art Criticism* 57, no. 2 (1999): 200. Davies holds a different view of the ontology of rock music. Davies maintains that rock songs (which can be structurally identified) are works that are very "thin"; in other words, they have few properties. See Davies, *Musical Works and Performances*, 16. If one accepts this view, then one must place much more evaluative emphasis upon the qualities of rock performances.

52 The Johnny Otis Show, "Willie and the Hand Jive" (Capital Records, 1958).

53 Roman Ingarden, *The Literary Work of Art*, trans. Grabowicz. (Evanston, IL: Northwestern University Press, 1973).

54 This synopsis of Ingarden's view draws heavily from my entry, "Phenomenology," in my *Key Terms in Philosophy of Art*.

55 When we evaluate a groove in a work, we must first adequately concretize it. How do we know if we have effectively done this? One thought is that we have adequately concretized it once we begin to comprehend how the various elements fit together.

56 Although we have not considered performing grooves much here, I will venture a guess that in order for Ringo (or anyone) to successfully strike those notes slightly earlier so as to generate a forward-leaning groove, he must be cognizant of the target leaning-forward feel—that feel will be his "imagined" goal on the basis of which to adjust the timing of those notes. For a drummer, at least in my experience, endeavoring to perform a particular groove has quite a bit to do with grasping a particular, embodied feel. It involves finding a particular posture and bodily movement routine. In aiming for a groove achieved in a previous performance, the drummer may recall the posture and movements, and she attempts to embody these while counting off the song. This is to leave the analytical approach far behind.

Bibliography

Baugh, Bruce. "Prolegomena to Any Aesthetics of Rock Music," *The Journal of Aesthetics and Art Criticism* 51 (1993): 23–9.

—"Music for the Young at Heart," *The Journal of Aesthetics and Art Criticism* 53, no. 1 (Winter, 1995): 81–3.

Beardsley, Monroe, C. *The Aesthetic Point of View*, ed. M. Wreen and D. Callen. Ithaca, NY: Cornell University Press, 1982.

Beatles, The. *Anthology*. Capital, 2003. DVD. Originally realeased in 1995.

Bell, Clive. *Art*. Oxford: Oxford University Press, 1987 (1914).

Bermudez, José Luis. "Nonconceptual Content: From Perceptual Experience to Subpersonal Computational States." In *Essays on Nonconceptual Content*, ed. York H. Gunther, 183–216. Cambridge, MA: MIT Press, 2003.

Bourdieu, Pierre, *Distinction: A Social Critique of the Judgement of Taste*. Translated by R. Nice. Cambridge, MA: Harvard University Press, 1984 (1979).

—"The Historical Genesis of a Pure Aesthetic," *The Journal of Aesthetics and Art Criticism* 46 (1987): 201–10.

Block, Ned. "Troubles with Functionalism." In *Readings in Philosophy of Psychology*, volume 1, ed. N. Block. Cambridge, MA: Harvard University Press, 1980.

—"Qualia." In *A Companion to the Philosophy of Mind*, edited by Samuel Guttenplan, 514–20. Oxford: Blackwell, 1996.

—"On a Confusion About a Function of Consciousness." In *The Nature of Consciousness*, eds N. Block, O. Flanagan and G. Guzeldere, 375–415. Cambridge, MA: MIT Press, 1998.

—"Mental Paint." In *Reflections and Replies: Essays on the Philosophy of Tyler Burge*, eds M. Hahn and B. Ramberg. Cambridge, MA: MIT Press, 2003.

—"Review of Alva Noë, Action in Perception," *Journal of Philosophy* CII, no. 5 (2005): 259–72.

Brown, Lee B. "The Theory of Jazz Music; 'It Don't Mean a Thing ...'" *The Journal of Aesthetics and Art Criticism* 49, no. 2 (1991): 115–27.

Byrne, Alex. "Intentionalism Defended," *The Philosophical Review* 110, no. 2 (2001): 199–240.

Carman, Taylor. "Sensation, Judgment, and the Phenomenal Field." In *The Cambridge Companion to Merleau-Ponty*, eds T. Carman and M. Hansen. Cambridge: Cambridge University Press, 2005.

—*Merleau-Ponty*. London and New York: Routledge, 2008.

Carroll, Noel. *Philosophy of Art* London and New York: Routledge, 1999.

Carroll-Phelan, B. and Hampson, P. J. "Multiple Components of the Perception of Musical Sequences: A Cognitive Neuroscience Analysis and Some Implications for Auditory Imagery," *Music Perception* no. 13 (1996): 517–61.

Chalmers, David J. *The Conscious Mind*. Oxford: Oxford University Press, 1996.

—"Facing up to the Problem of Consciousness." In *Explaining Consciousness*, ed. Jonathan Shear, 10–30. Cambridge, MA: MIT Press, 1997.

—"The Representational Character of Experience." In *The Future for Philosophy*, ed. Brian Leiter. Oxford: Oxford University Press, 2004.

Clarke, E. F. "The Perception of Expressive Timing in Music," *Psychological Research* 51 (1989): 2–9.

Clayton, Martin, Sager, Rebecca, and Will, Udo. "In Time With The Music: The Concept of Entrainment and its Significance for Ethnomusicology," *ESEM Counterpoint* II (2005): 3–75.

Collingwood, R. G. *The Principles of Art*. New York: Oxford University Press, 1958 (1938).

Crane, Tim. "The Intentional Structure of Consciousness." In *Consciousness*, eds Quentin Smith and Aleksandar Jokic, 33–56. Oxford: Oxford University Press, 2003.

Davies, Stephen. *Musical Works and Performances*. Oxford: Oxford University Press, 2001.

—"Rock Versus Classical Music," *Journal of Aesthetics and Art Criticism* 57, no. 2 (1999): 193–204.

DeBellis, Mark. "The Representational Content of Musical Experience," *Philosophy and Phenomenological Research* LI, no. 2 (1991): 303–24.

—*Music and Conceptualization*. Cambridge: Cambridge University Press, 1995.

Dennett, Daniel C. "Quining Qualia." In *Philosophy of Mind: Classical and Contemporary Readings*, ed. David J. Chalmers, 226–46. Oxford: Oxford University Press, 2002.

Deutsch, Diana, ed. *The Psychology of Music*. San Diego: Elsevier, 1982.

Dewey, John. *Art as Experience*, New York: Perigee, 1980 (1934).

Dretsky, Fred. *Knowledge and the Flow of Information*. Cambridge, MA: MIT Press, 1981.

Dreyfus, Hubert. "Responses." In *Heidegger, Coping, and Cognitive Science: Essays in Honor of Hubert L. Dreyfus,* Volume 2, eds Mark A. Wrathall and Jeff Malpas. Cambridge, MA and London: MIT Press, 2000.

—"Merleau-Ponty and Recent Cognitive Science." In *The Cambridge Companion to Merleau-Ponty*, eds Taylor Carman and Mark Hansen. Cambridge: Cambridge University Press, 2005.

Embree, L. "Merleau-Ponty's Examination of Gestalt Psychology," *Research in Phenomenology* 10 (1980): 89–121

Emerick, Geoff and Massey, Howard. *Here, There and Everywhere: My Life Recording the Music of the Beatles*. New York: Penguin Books, 2006.

Evans, Gareth. *The Varieties of Reference*. Oxford: Oxford University Press, 1982.

Feld, Steven. "Aesthetics as Iconicity of Style (Uptown Title); Or, (Downtown Title) 'Lift-Up-Over Sounding': Getting into the Kaluli Groove." In *Musical Grooves*, eds Charles Keil and Steven Feld. Tucson, AZ: Fenstra, 2005.

Fodor, Jerry. *The Modularity of Mind*. Cambridge, MA: MIT Press, 1983.

Fry, Roger. *Cézanne: A Study of His Development*. New York: Macmillan, 1927.

Gallagher, S. "Representation and deliberate action." *Houston Studies in Cognitive Science* 1 (2000). http://www.hfac.uh.edu/hscs/commentators/gallagher.htm.

Gallagher, S. and Zahavi, D. *The Phenomenological Mind: An Introduction to Philosophy of Mind and Cognitive Science*. London and New York: Routledge, 2008.

Gracyk, Theodore. *Rhythm and Noise: an Aesthetics of Rock*. London and New York: I. B. Tauris, 1996.

—*Listening to Popular Music: Or, How I Learned to Stop Worrying and Love Led Zeppelin*. Ann Arbor: University of Michigan Press, 2007.

Gracyk, Theodore and Kania, Andrew, eds *The Routledge Companion to Philosophy and Music*. London and New York: Routledge, 2011.

Harman, Gilbert. "The Intrinsic Quality of Experience," *Philosophical Perspectives 4, Action Theory and Philosophy of Mind* (1990): 31–52.

Hass, Lawrence. *Merleau-Ponty's Philosophy*. Bloomington and Indianapolis: Indiana University Press, 2008.

Heidegger, Martin. *Being and Time*. Trans. John Macquarrie and Edward Robinson. New York: Harper Perennial Modern Classics, 2008 (1927).

Ingarden, Roman. *The Literary Work of Art*. Trans. G. G. Grabowicz. Evanston, IL: Northwestern University Press, 1973.

—"Phenomenological Aesthetics: An Attempt at Defining Its Range," *The Journal of Aesthetics and Art Criticism* 33, no. 3 (1975): 257–69.

Iyer, Vijay. "Microstructures of Feel, Macrostructures of Sound: Embodied Cognition in West African and African-American Musics." PhD diss, University of California, Berkeley, 1998.

—"Embodied Mind, Situated Cognition, and Expressive Microtiming in African-American Music," *Music Perception* 19, no. 3 (2002): 387–414.

Keil, Charles. "Theory of Participatory Discrepancies: a Progress Report," *Ethnomusicology* 39, no. 1, Special Issue: *Participatory Discrepancies* (Winter 1995): 1–19.

—"Participatory Discrepancies and the Power of Music." In *Musical Grooves*, eds Charles Keil and Steven Feld. Tucson, AZ: Fenstra, 2005.

Keil, Charles and Feld, Steven. *Musical Grooves*. Tucson, AZ: Fenstra, 2005.

Kelly, Sean D. "Grasping at Straws: Motor Intentionality and the Cognitive Science of Skilled Behavior." In *Heidegger, Coping, and Cognitive Science: Essays in Honor of Hubert L. Dreyfus*, volume 2, eds Mark A. Wrathall and Jeff Malpas. Cambridge, MA and London: MIT Press, 2000.

—"Merleau-Ponty on the Body: The Logic of Motor Intentional Activity," *Ratio XV*, 4 (2002): 376–91.

—"Edmund Husserl and Phenomenology." In *The Blackwell Guide to Continental Philosophy*, eds Robert C. Solomon and David Sherman, 112–42. Oxford: Blackwell, 2003.

—"Seeing Things in Merleau-Ponty." In *The Cambridge Companion to Merleau-Ponty*, eds Taylor Carman and Mark Hansen. Cambridge: Cambridge University Press, 2005.

Kennick, W. E. "Art and the Ineffable," *Journal of Philosophy* 58, 12 (1961): 309–20.

Kernfeld, Barry. "Groove (i)." *The New Grove Dictionary of Jazz*, 2nd edn. *Grove Music Online. Oxford Music Online.* Oxford: Oxford University Press. http://www.oxfordmusiconline.com/subscriber/article/grove/music/J582400 (accessed January 25, 2014).

Koffka, Kurt. "Perception: An Introduction to the Gestalt-Theorie," *Psychological Bulletin* 19 (1922): 531–85.

Köhler, Wolfgang. *Gestalt Psychology.* New York: Mentor Books, 1959.

Lerdahl, Fred and Jackendoff, Ray. *A Generative Theory of Tonal Music.* Cambridge, MA and London: MIT Press, 1983.

Lewisohn, Mark. *The Complete Beatles Recording Sessions: The Official Story of the Abbey Road Years 1962–1970,* repr. edn. New York: Sterling, 2013.

London, Justin. "The Fine Art of Repetition: Essays in the Philosophy of Music; Language, Music, and Mind," *Music Theory Spectrum* 16 (1994): 269–75.

—"Pulse." *Grove Music Online. Oxford Music Online.* Oxford University Press. http://www.oxfordmusiconline.com/subscriber/article/grove/music/45964 (accessed May 21, 2014).

—"Rhythm." *Grove Music Online. Oxford Music Online.* Oxford University Press. http://www.oxfordmusiconline.com/subscriber/article/grove/music/45963 (accessed May 21, 2014).

—*Hearing in Time: Psychological Aspects of Musical Meter*, 2nd edn. Oxford: Oxford University Press, 2012.

Mathiesen, Thomas. "Ancient Greek music." *The Oxford Companion to Music. Oxford Music Online.* Oxford University Press, http://www.oxfordmusiconline.com/subscriber/article/opr/t114/e260 (accessed May 21, 2014).

Matthews, Eric. *The Philosophy of Merleau-Ponty.* Montreal and Kingston: McGill-Queen's University Press, 2002.

Merleau-Ponty, Maurice. "The Film and the New Psychology." In *Sense and Non-Sense*, eds H. L. Dreyfus and P. A. Dreyfus. Evanston, IL: Northwestern University Press, 1964.

—*In Praise of Philosophy and Other Essays*. Trans. John Wild, James Edie, and John O'Neill. Evanston, IL: Northwestern University Press, 1970.

—"Cézanne's Doubt." In *The Merleau-Ponty Aesthetics Reader*, ed. Galen A. Johnson. Evanston, IL: Northwestern University Press, 1993 (1945).

—*Phenomenology of Perception*. Trans. Donald A. Landes. London and New York: Routledge, 2012 (1945).

Middleton, Richard. "Form." In *Key Terms in Popular Music and Culture*, eds Bruce Horner and Thom Swiss. Oxford: Blackwell, 1999.

Milner, A. David and Goodale, Melvyn A. *The Visual Brain in Action*. Oxford: Oxford University Press, 1996.

Mitscherling, Jeffrey Anthony. *Roman Ingarden's Ontology and Aesthetics*. Ottawa: University of Ottawa Press, 1997.

Nagel, Thomas. "What Is It Like to Be a Bat?" *Philosophical Review* 83 (1974): 435–50.

Nietzsche, Friedrich Wilhelm. *The Gay Science*, ed. Bernard Williams, trans. Josefine Nauckhoff. Cambridge and New York: Cambridge University Press, 2001.

Noë, Alva. *Action in Perception*. Cambridge, MA: MIT Press, 2004.

Peacocke, Christopher. *Sense and Content*. Oxford: Oxford University Press, 1983.

—"Perceptual Content." In *Themes from Kaplan*, eds J. Almog, J. Perry, and H. Wettstein, 297–329. New York and Oxford: Oxford University Press, 1989.

—*A Study of Concepts*. Cambridge, MA: MIT Press, 1992.

—"Nonconceptual Content Defended," *Philosophy and Phenomenological Research* LVIII, no. 2 (1998): 381–8.

—"Does Perception Have a Nonconceptual Content?" *Journal of Philosophy* 98, no. 5 (2001): 239–64.

—"Scenarios, Concepts, and Perception." In *Essays on Nonconceptual Content*, ed. York H. Gunther, 107–32. Cambridge: Cambridge University Press, 2003.

Plato. *The Republic*. Trans. C. D. C. Reeve and G. M. A. Grube. Indianapolis and Cambridge: Hackett, 1992.

Prögler, J. A. "Searching for Swing: Participatory Discrepancies in the Jazz Rhythm Section," *Ethnomusicology*, 39, no. 1, Special Issue: *Participatory Discrepancies* (Winter, 1995): 21–54.

Raffman, Diana. *Language, Music, and Mind*. Cambridge, MA and London: MIT Press, 1993.

Rey, Georges. Review of *Language, Music, and Mind*, *The Philosophical Review* 106 (1997): 641–5.

Robinson, Howard. *Perception*. London and New York: Routledge, 1994.

Roholt, Tiger. "Groove: The Phenomenology of Musical Nuance." PhD diss, Columbia University, 2007.

—"*Musical* Musical Nuance," *The Journal of Aesthetics and Art Criticism* 68, no. 1 (Winter 2010): 1–10.

—"Continental Philosophy and Music." In *The Routledge Companion to Philosophy and Music*, eds Theodore Gracyk and Andrew Kania. London and New York: Routledge, 2011.

—"In Praise of Ambiguity: Merleau-Ponty and Musical Subtlety," *Contemporary Aesthetics* 11 (2013), http://www.contempaesthetics. org/newvolume/pages/article.php?articleID=669 (accessed May 21, 2014).

—*Key Terms in Philosophy of Art*. London and New York: Bloomsbury Academic, 2013.

Rouse, Joseph. "Coping and Its Contrasts." In *Heidegger, Coping, and Cognitive Science: Essays in Honor of Hubert L. Dreyfus*, volume 2, eds Mark A. Wrathall and Jeff Malpas. Cambridge, MA and London: MIT Press, 2000.

Shepard, Roger. "Stream Segregation and Ambiguity in Audition." In *Music, Cognition, and Computerized Sound: An Introduction to Psychoacoustics*, ed. P. R. Cook. Cambridge, MA: MIT Press, 1999.

Shusterman, Richard. *Performing Live: Aesthetic Alternatives for the Ends of Art*. Ithaca, NY and London: Cornell University Press, 2000.

—"Don't Believe the Hype." In *Performing Live: Aesthetic Alternatives for the Ends of Art*. Ithaca and London: Cornell University Press, 2000.

—*Body Consciousness: A Philosophy of Mindfulness and Somaesthetics*. Cambridge and New York: Cambridge University Press, 2008.

—*Thinking Through the Body: Essays in Somaesthetics*. Cambridge and New York: Cambridge University Press, 2012.

Spackman, John. "Expressiveness, Ineffability, and Nonconceptuality," *The Journal of Aesthetics and Art Criticism* 70:3, Summer 2012.

Stoljar, Daniel. "The Argument from Diaphanousness." In *Language, Mind, and World: Special Issue of the Canadian Journal of Philosophy,* eds R. Stainton, M. Escurdia, and C. Viger, 2004.

Todd, Neill P. M., O'Boyle, Donald J., and others. "A Sensory-Motor Theory of Rhythm, Time Perception, and Beat Induction," *Journal of New Music Research* 28, no. 1 (1999): 5–28.

Tye, Michael. *Ten Problems of Consciousness*. Cambridge, MA: MIT Press, 1995.

—"Knowing What It Is Like: The Ability Hypothesis and the Knowledge Argument." In *Reality and Humean Supervenience*, eds G. Preyer and F. Siebert. Lanham, MD: Rowman and Littlefield, 2000.

—*Consciousness, Color, and Content*. Cambridge, MA: MIT, 2002.

Wittgenstein, Ludwig. *The Blue and Brown Books*, 2nd edn. Oxford: Blackwell, 1998.

Wrathall, Mark A. "Motives, Reasons, and Causes." In *The Cambridge Companion to Merleau-Ponty*, eds T. Carman and M. Hansen, 111–28. Cambridge: Cambridge University Press, 2005.

Wrathall, Mark A. and Malpas Jeff, eds. *Heidegger, Coping, and Cognitive Science: Essays in Honor of Hubert L. Dreyfus*, volume 2. Cambridge, MA and London: MIT Press, 2000.

Discography

Beatles, The. "Love Me Do" (Ringo on drums), *Past Masters*. EMI, 2009, compact disc.

—"Love Me Do" (Andy White on drums), *Please Please Me*. EMI, 1963, compact disc.

—"All My Lovin", *With the Beatles*. Parlophone/Capitol, 1990, compact disc.

Brandy. "What About Us?" *Full Moon*. Urban Atlantic, 2004, compact disc.

Dr. Dre. "Forgot about Dre," 2001. *Aftermath*, Interscope, 1999.

Ford, Tennessee Ernie. "Sixteen Tons," *Vintage Collections Series*. EMI Special Products, 1997, compact disc.

Gnarls Barkley. "Crazy," *St. Elsewhere*. Atlantic, 2006, compact disc.

Johnny Otis Show, The. "Willie and the Hand Jive." Capital Records, 1958.

Led Zeppelin. "Blackdog," *Led Zeppelin IV*. Atlantic, 1994, compact disc. Originally released in 1971.

Lorde. "Royals," *Pure Heroine*. Universal Music Group, 2013.

P. Diddy. "Bad Boy for Life," *The Saga Continues*. Bad Boy, 2001, compact disc.

Robbins, Marty. "El Paso," *Gunfighter Ballads and Trail Songs*. Sony, 1999, compact disc.

Sinatra, F. and Basie, C. "Fly Me to the Moon: In Other Words," *Sinatra at the Sands*. Warner Bros/WEA, 1998, compact disc. Originally released in 1966.

Tame Impala. "Elephant," *Lonerism*. Modular Recordings, 2012.

Sly and The Family Stone. "Thank You (Falettinme Be Mice Elf Agin)," *Greatest Hits*. Epic Records, 1970.

Vincent, Gene. "Race with the Devil," *The Screaming End: The Best Of Gene Vincent*. Razor and Tie, 1997, compact disc. Originally released in 1956.

Winehouse, Amy. "Back to Black," *Back to Black*. Republic, 2007, compact disc.

Index